Scott Foresman - Addison Wesley

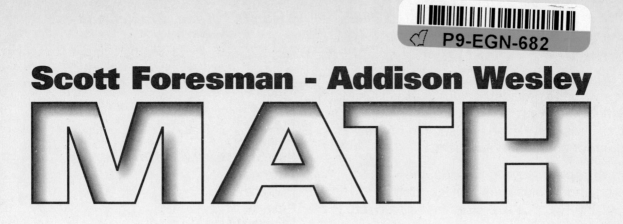

Practice Workbook

Grade 3

Scott Foresman - Addison Wesley

Editorial Offices: Menlo Park, California • Glenview, Illinois
Sales Offices: Reading, Massachusetts • Atlanta, Georgia • Glenview, Illinois
Carrollton, Texas • Menlo Park, California

http://www.sf.aw.com

Overview

The *Practice Workbook* provides additional practice on the concept or concepts taught in each core lesson.

For Learn and Explore lessons, the worksheets provide additional exercises that reflect those in the Connect section and/or the Skills and Reasoning section of the student edition Practice sets.

For Problem Solving lessons, the worksheets closely mirror the Problem Solving Practice exercises in the student edition.

The *Practice Workbook* also includes Section Reviews that supplement the Section Review pages in the student edition. These Section Review worksheets also provide Mixed Review problems (from previous sections of the student edition). Cumulative Review worksheets are included at the end of each chapter to provide a comprehensive review of skills covered up through that chapter.

ISBN 0-201-31244-1

Copyright © Addison Wesley Longman, Inc.

Printed in the United States of America

10 – BW – 02 01 00

Contents

Chapter 4: Subtracting Whole Numbers and Money

Chapter 5: Multiplication Concepts and Facts

Chapter 6: More Multiplication Facts

Chapter 7: Division Concepts and Facts

Chapter 8: Using Geometry

Name _____

Reading Pictographs

Use the pictograph to answer each question.

Sleepy Animals

Animal	Average Hours of Sleep a Day
Armadillo	🛏🛏🛏🛏🛏🛏🛏🛏🛏⌐
Cat	🛏🛏🛏🛏🛏🛏⌐
Hamster	🛏🛏🛏🛏🛏🛏🛏
Koala	🛏🛏🛏🛏🛏🛏🛏🛏🛏🛏🛏
Lemur	🛏🛏🛏🛏🛏🛏🛏🛏
Opossum	🛏🛏🛏🛏🛏🛏🛏🛏🛏⌐
Pig	🛏🛏🛏🛏🛏⌐
Sloth	🛏🛏🛏🛏🛏🛏🛏🛏🛏🛏
Spiny anteater	🛏🛏🛏🛏🛏🛏
Squirrel	🛏🛏🛏🛏🛏🛏🛏

🛏 = 2 hours of sleep

1. Which animal sleeps the most? _____

2. Which two animals get the same amount of sleep each day.

_____

3. Which animal sleeps 16 hours per day? _____

4. How many more hours per day does a
   koala sleep than a pig? _____

5. How many animals sleep more than 12 hours? _____

6. Which animal sleeps exactly 12 hours? _____

7. Which animal sleeps the least? _____

8. Suppose a dog sleeps 6 hours per day. How
   many symbols would the dog have? _____

Name _____

Reading Bar Graphs

Use the bar graph to answer each question.

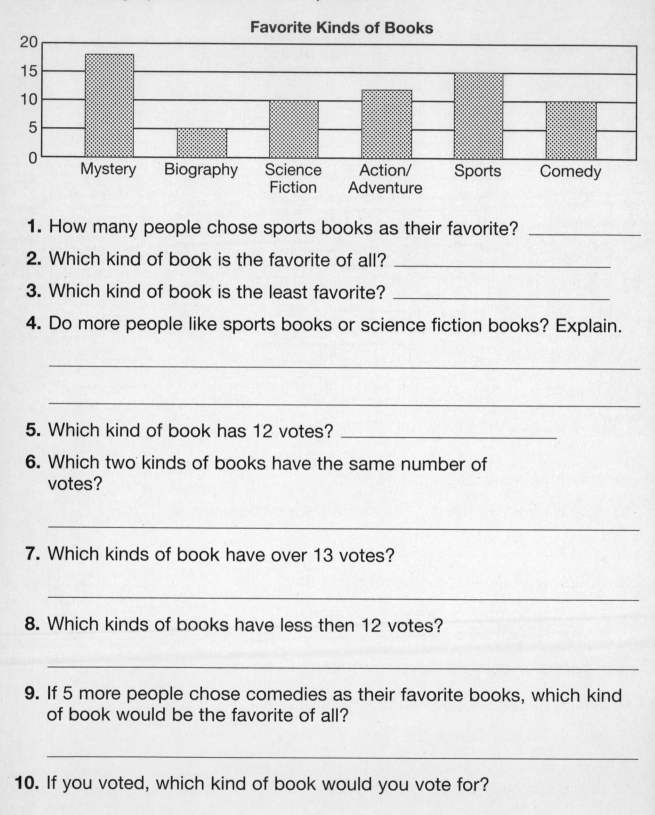

Favorite Kinds of Books

1. How many people chose sports books as their favorite? _____

2. Which kind of book is the favorite of all? _____

3. Which kind of book is the least favorite? _____

4. Do more people like sports books or science fiction books? Explain.

   _____

   _____

5. Which kind of book has 12 votes? _____

6. Which two kinds of books have the same number of
   votes?

   _____

7. Which kinds of book have over 13 votes?

   _____

8. Which kinds of books have less then 12 votes?

   _____

9. If 5 more people chose comedies as their favorite books, which kind
   of book would be the favorite of all?

   _____

10. If you voted, which kind of book would you vote for?

   _____

Reading Line Graphs

Use the line graph to answer each question.

A hot tub holds many gallons of water. Cold water is put into the tub and warmed slowly. This graph shows how long it will take for water to reach 100 degrees. You don't want the water in a hot tub much warmer than 100 degrees or it would be too hot.

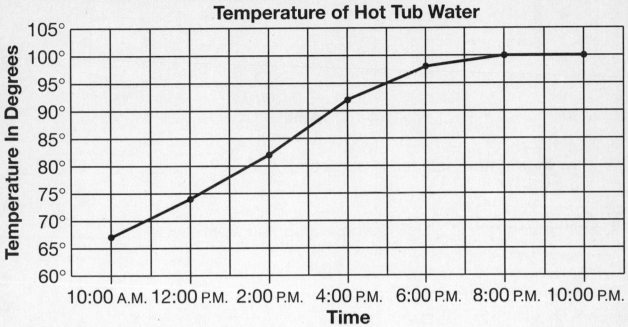

Temperature of Hot Tub Water

1. How hot was the water at 10:00 A.M.? _____

2. At what time was the water about 74°? _____

3. How many degrees did the water change between 10:00 A.M. and 12:00 P.M.? _____

4. How many degrees did the water change between 12:00 P.M. and 2:00 P.M.? _____

5. At what time was the water about 92°? _____

6. When did the water reach 100°? _____

7. What happened to the temperature of the water between 8:00 P.M. and 10:00 P.M.? _____

Name _____

Analyze Word Problems:
Introduction to Problem Solving

Plan how you will solve each problem. Then solve.

Monthly Rainfall

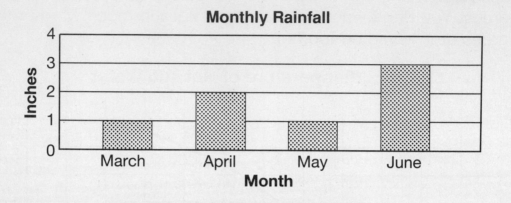

1. How much more rain fell in June than in April? _____

2. How much rain in all fell during March and April? _____

3. How much total rain fell in all four months? _____

4. If there was 2 inches more rain in July than there was in April, how much rain was there in July? _____

5. Which 2 months combined had the same amount of rainfall as there was in April? _____

6. Which month had twice as much rain as March? _____

7. Which month had three times as much rain as March? _____

Name _____

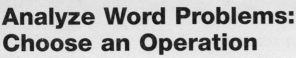
Analyze Word Problems:
Choose an Operation

Choose the number sentence you would use to solve. Explain.

1. Sam owns 3 lizards and 2 cats. How many pets does
   Sam own?

   a. 3 + 2 = 5   **b.** 3 − 2 = 1

   _____

   _____

2. Lisa moved 9 boxes. On Monday, she unpacked 5
   boxes. How many more boxes are left to unpack?

   a. 9 + 5 = 14   **b.** 9 − 5 = 4

   _____

3. Tony baked 4 dozen muffins in the morning and 3 dozen
   more in the afternoon. How many dozen muffins did he
   bake in one day?

   a. 4 + 3 = 7   **b.** 4 − 3 = 1

   _____

Write which operation you would use. Then solve.

4. Sarah bought 10 cherries on Saturday. On Sunday, she
   ate 5. How many cherries does she have now?

   _____

5. Francis bought 7 cans of beans and 6 cans of corn. How
   many cans did he buy?

   _____

6. Judy is in a 10-kilometer road race. She has run 6
   kilometers already. How many more kilometers will
   she run?

   _____

Exploring Algebra: What's the Rule?

1. A rule describes what to do to the **In** number
to get the **Out** number. What is the rule? _____

In	8	9	10	11	12	13
Out	5	6	7	8	9	10

Complete each table. Write the rule for each.

2.

In	4	6	2	5	10	8
Out	8	10	6			

Rule: _____

3.

In	8	4	3	5	11	6
Out	6	2	1			

Rule: _____

4.

In	10	7	6	4	12	3
Out	15	12	11			

Rule: _____

5.

In	9	11	8	4	6	7
Out	5	7	4			

Rule: _____

Name _____

Review and Practice

(Lesson 1) Use the pictograph to answer each question.

1. How many letters were received?

_____

2. Which type of mail was received

the most? _____

3. How many symbols would there

be if 20 greeting cards were

received? _____

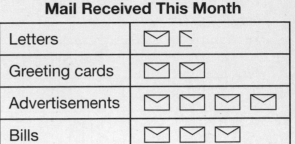

Mail Received This Month

Letters	
Greeting cards	
Advertisements	
Bills	

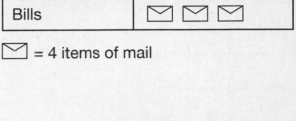

= 4 items of mail

(Lesson 2) Use the bar graph to answer each question.

4. Which fruit was the least favorite?

_____

5. Which fruit did 10 people vote for?

_____

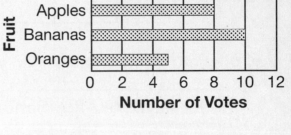

Favorite Kinds of Fruit

6. How many more voted for apples than oranges? _____

(Lesson 3) Use the line graph to answer each question.

7. In what year were the most books

checked out? _____

8. In what year were only 2,000

books checked out? _____

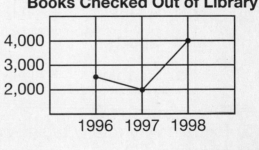

Books Checked Out of Library

(Lesson 5) Tell which operation you would use. Then solve.

9. There are 12 boys in the class. 8 have brown

eyes. How many do not have brown eyes? _____

(Mixed Review) Add or subtract.

10. $6 + 9 =$ _____   **11.** $8 - 6 =$ _____   **12.** $7 + 7 =$ _____

Name _____

Exploring Organizing Data

1. This tally table shows students' votes for their favorite colors. Write the number of students who voted for each color.

Favorite Colors		
Color	**Tally**	**Number**
a. Blue	ЖЖ	
b. Purple	ЖЖ ||||	
c. Red	|	
d. Green	ЖЖ	
e. Yellow	ЖЖ |	

2. Complete the tally table.

Our Favorite After-School Activities		
Activity	**Tally**	**Number**
a. Bike Riding	|||	
b. Crafts	ЖЖ	
c. Sports	ЖЖ ||	
d. Reading	||||	

3. Explain why a tally table is a useful way to present survey results.

_____

_____

Exploring Making Pictographs

Here are two different ways to show data using a pictograph.

Francie's Way

Chuck's Way

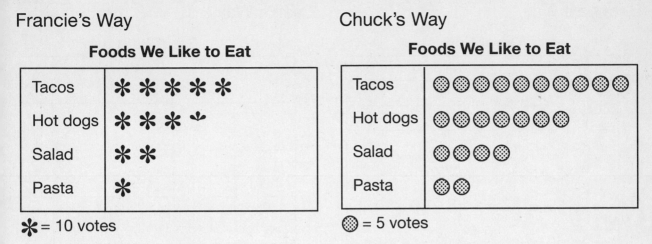

Foods We Like to Eat

Tacos	✳ ✳ ✳ ✳ ✳
Hot dogs	✳ ✳ ✳ ✴
Salad	✳ ✳
Pasta	✳

✳ = 10 votes

Foods We Like to Eat

Tacos	◉◉◉◉◉◉◉◉◉◉
Hot dogs	◉◉◉◉◉◉◉
Salad	◉◉◉◉
Pasta	◉◉

◉ = 5 votes

1. Describe one difference between the 2 pictographs.

_____

2. Students like to study in different places. Complete the
   pictograph. Use the data in the table.

Where Students Like to Study

Library	𝍷𝍷𝍷𝍷𝍷 𝍷
At a desk	𝍷𝍷𝍷𝍷𝍷 𝍷𝍷𝍷𝍷𝍷 𝍷𝍷𝍷𝍷𝍷 𝍷
On the bed	𝍷𝍷𝍷𝍷𝍷 𝍷𝍷𝍷
On the floor	𝍷𝍷𝍷𝍷𝍷 𝍷𝍷𝍷𝍷𝍷
Other	𝍷𝍷𝍷𝍷𝍷 𝍷𝍷𝍷𝍷𝍷 𝍷𝍷

Where Students Like to Study

Library	■ ■ ■
At a desk	
On the bed	
On the floor	
Other	

■ = 2 students

3. Suppose each symbol in the pictograph above
   represented 3 students. How many symbols
   would there be for "Other"?

   _____

Name _____

Exploring Making Bar Graphs

Here are two bar graphs that show the same data.

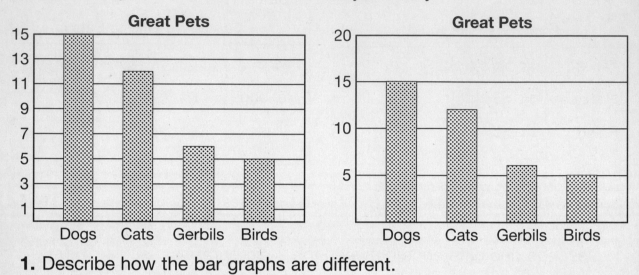

Brianna's Way

Elijah's Way

1. Describe how the bar graphs are different.

_____

Use the data in the table to complete the bar graph.

Day	Number of Books Sold
Monday	6
Tuesday	9
Wednesday	3
Thursday	12
Friday	9

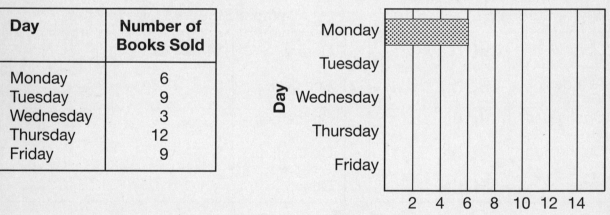

2. Complete the bar graph.

3. How many more books were sold on Tuesday than Monday? _____

4. On what days were the same number of books sold?

_____

Name _____

Decision Making

Suppose the members of your class are
collecting containers for recycling. The table
shows the kind and number of containers
collected.

Items Collected	
Aluminum cans	80
Milk containers	45
Soft drinks	65
Large glass	50
Small glass	15

1. Look at the data. Is the information best
   suited for a bar graph or a pictograph?
   Explain.

   _____

   _____

2. What would you title the graph?

   _____

3. Use the space provided to make a graph. If you make a pictograph,
   let each symbol show 10 containers. If you make a bar graph, make a
   scale by counting by 10s.

4. What if each symbol in your pictograph showed 5 containers? Or,
   what if you made your scale in your bar graph by counting by 5s?
   How would your graph be different?

   _____

   _____

   _____

Analyze Strategies: Look for a Pattern

Look for a pattern to help you solve each problem.

1. If the pattern continues, which shape should come next? _____

○ □ △ ○ □ △ ○

2. If the pattern continues, which shape should come next? _____

● ○ ○ ● ○ ○ ●

3. What are the next 3 numbers?

2, 6, 10, 14, _____, _____, _____

4. What are the next 3 numbers?

10, 20, 30, 40, _____, _____, _____

5. Andrea says, "The next picture in this pattern should be a spoon." Do you agree or disagree? Explain.

🍴 🔪 🥄 🥄 🍴 🔪 🥄 🥄 🍴 🔪 🥄

_____

Look for a pattern or use any strategy to help you solve each problem.

6. Members of the Sal Pal Club receive member cards with their member I.D. number. The first member's number is 111. The second member's number is 121. The third and fourth members' numbers are 131 and 141.

a. What I.D. numbers should be given to the next 2 members? _____

b. What two I.D. numbers could the tenth member receive that would still fit the pattern? Explain.

_____

_____

Review and Practice

(Lesson 7) Complete the tally table.

1. Number of pets in the homes
of Mr. Gregory's third grade class:

2, 1, 0, 2, 2, 0, 0, 1, 2, 1, 0, 0, 2, 1,

1, 2, 0, 0, 1, 1, 1, 1, 0

Pets	Tally	Number
0		
1		
2		

(Lesson 8) Use the data in the table. Complete the pictograph.

2.

My Favorite Flavor	
Peppermint	5
Chocolate	15
Butterscotch	7

My Favorite Flavor

Peppermint	
Chocolate	
Butterscotch	

Key   = 2

(Lesson 9) Use the data in the table. Complete the bar graph.

3.

Warren's Reading Time	
Day of Week	Minutes
Monday	30
Tuesday	20
Wednesday	15
Thursday	35

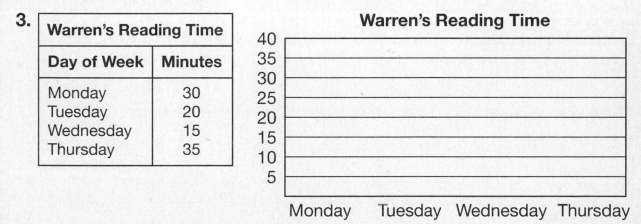

Warren's Reading Time

(Lesson 11) Solve. Use any strategy.

4. Leandra is learning to play the trombone. She
increases her practice time by 3 minutes each
day. Monday she practiced 8 minutes. How
many minutes will she practice on Friday?   _____

(Mixed Review) Add or subtract.

5. $6 + 9 =$ _____   6. $16 - 9 =$ _____   7. $5 + 8 =$ _____

Cumulative Review

(Chapter 1 Lessons 1 and 8) Use the data to complete the pictograph.

1.

Number of Rooms in Home	
Marlene	5
Patrick	4
Lois	6

Number of Rooms in Home

Marlene	
Patrick	
Lois	

Key:

= 2 rooms

2. How many symbols would you use
   to represent 11 rooms?   _____

(Chapter 1 Lessons 2 and 9) Use the data to complete the bar graph.

3.

Dogs at Veterinarian's Office	
Day of Week	**Number of Dogs**
Monday	3
Tuesday	1
Wednesday	5

Dogs at Veterinarian's Office

Day of the Week: M, T, W

Number of Dogs: 1 2 3 4 5 6

4. How many dogs were seen by the veterinarian on all three days?

   _____

(Chapter 1 Lesson 3) Use the line graph to answer the questions.

5. How many children played soccer in 1996?

   _____

6. Do you think the number of children playing
   soccer in 1999 will be greater than in 1998?
   Explain.

   _____

   _____

Number of Children Playing Soccer

300
250
200
150
100

1996 1997 1998 1999
Years

(Facts Review) Add or subtract.

7. $13 - 7 =$ _____   8. $6 + 8 =$ _____

9. $7 + 5 =$ _____   10. $7 - 4 =$ _____

Place Value Through Hundreds

Write each number in standard form.

1. _____

2. _____

3. forty-nine _____

4. thirteen _____

5. 200 + 70 + 8 _____

6. 100 + 30 + 2 _____

7. 300 + 30 _____

8. sixty-five _____

9. 200 + 2 _____

10. 500 + 40 + 5 _____

11. two hundred sixty-two _____

12. three hundred forty-seven _____

Write the word name for each number.

13. 93 _____

14. 348 _____

15. 102 _____

16. 56 _____

17. 210 _____

18. 312 _____

19. 452 _____

20. 205 _____

21. In the number 349, which digit has the least value? Explain.

_____

22. To write the number three hundred ten, do you need a 0? Explain.

_____

23. Write the numbers five hundred ten and five hundred one.

_____

Name _____

Exploring Place-Value Relationships
Complete.

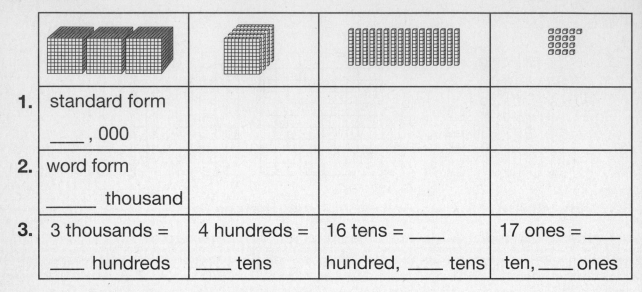

1.	standard form _____ , 000			
2.	word form _____ thousand			
3.	3 thousands = _____ hundreds	4 hundreds = _____ tens	16 tens = _____ hundred, _____ tens	17 ones = _____ ten, _____ ones

Write each number in standard form.

4. _____

5. _____

Complete the table.

	Number	Number of Ones	Number of Tens	Number of Hundreds
6.	100	100		
7.	700			7
8.	400		40	
9.	1,000	1,000		

10. How many ways can you write 600? Write them.

_____

11. How many ways can you write 5,000? Write them.

_____

Place Value Through Thousands

Write each number in standard form.

1. _____

2. _____

3. three thousand, four hundred seventeen _____

4. six thousand, seven hundred thirty-eight _____

5. 2,000 + 60 + 8 _____   **6.** 7,000 + 100 + 40 + 5 _____

Write the word name for each number.

7. 393 _____

8. 9,463 _____

9. 6,795 _____

Complete the table.

	Number	100 More	100 Less
10.	2,612		
11.	3,911		
12.	6,208		

13. Is 27 hundreds the same as 27 tens? Explain.

_____

14. Is 100 the same as 10 ones or 10 tens? _____

15. Choose a number greater than 1,000 and write it 3 ways.

_____

Place Value Through Hundred Thousands

Write each number in standard form.

1. twenty-nine thousand, five hundred sixteen _____

2. four hundred thirty-five thousand, seven hundred eight _____

3. three hundred seventy-two thousand, fifty-four _____

4. 20,000 + 9,000 + 700 + 80 + 1 _____

5. 900,000 + 50,000 + 1,000 + 70 + 5 _____

6. 700,000 + 2,000 + 400 + 80 + 2 _____

Write the value of each underlined digit.

7. 2̲3,045 _____   8. 56̲2,021 _____

9. 8̲03,096 _____   10. 451,38̲2 _____

11. 12,5̲38 _____   12. 837,03̲6 _____

13. 34,7̲89 _____   14. 89̲,123 _____

15. 3̲24,598 _____   16. 47̲8,654 _____

17. Which digit has the least value in 34,187? Explain.

_____

_____

18. How many thousands is 100,000? How many ten thousands?

_____

19. Using the digits 2, 4, and 6, write a number with a 4 in the hundred thousands place and a 2 in the hundreds place.

_____

20. Using the digits 1, 3, and 5 only once, write the greatest and least three-digit numbers you can.

_____

Analyze Strategies:
Make an Organized List

Make a list or use any strategy to help solve each.

1. Suppose Carlos wants to order 40 light bulbs for the
   factory. He can buy light bulbs in boxes of 4 or 8.
   How many ways could he order exactly 40 bulbs?

   a. List all possible ways he could order 40 light bulbs.

boxes of 8						
boxes of 4						

   b. How many ways are there? _____

2. Suppose Susan wants 49 boxes of light bulbs. She can
   order them in packs of 10 boxes or 1 box at a time. How
   many ways can she order 49 boxes?

   _____

   _____

   _____

3. Pamela has a red shirt and a white shirt, black pants and
   a yellow skirt. How many different outfits can she make?

   _____

4. Three students are waiting in line to buy a venus fly trap.
   Barb is behind Jan. Mike is first in line. In what order are

   the students standing? _____

5. Don and Carrie had 13 orders for plants in the last two
   days. If they had 5 orders yesterday, how many orders

   did they have today? _____

6. When would you make a list to solve a problem?

   _____

   _____

Name _____

Review and Practice

Vocabulary Choose the best number for each description.

_____ **1.** Standard form   **a.** 240

_____ **2.** Expanded form   **b.** 0, 1, 2, 3, 4, 5, 6, 7, 8, and 9

_____ **3.** Digits   **c.** 300 + 50 + 2

(Lesson 1) Write the word name for each number.

4. _____   **5.** _____

6. 246 _____   **7.** 80 + 2 _____

(Lesson 2) Write each missing value.

8. 60 ones = _____ tens   **9.** _____ ones = 3 hundreds

10. 70 tens = _____ hundreds   **11.** _____ tens = 600 ones

(Lesson 3) Write each number in standard form.

12. seven thousand three _____   **13.** 5,000 + 700 + 7 _____

(Lesson 4) Write the value of each underlined digit.

14. 235,641 _____   **15.** 899,002 _____

(Lesson 5) Make a list to help solve.

16. Kara needs $35 for an aquarium for 6 fish. How can she pay with the least ten and one dollar bills?

_____

(Mixed Review) Add or subtract.

17. 7 + 3 = _____   **18.** 16 − 7 = _____   **19.** 9 + 9 = _____

Comparing Numbers

Compare. Use <, >, or =.

1. 27 ◯ 24

2. 416 ◯ 925

3. 2,197 ◯ 3,208

4. 2,450 ◯ 450

5. 20 ◯ 311

6. 1,717 ◯ 7,171

7. 624 ◯ 620

8. 329 ◯ 923

Write "is less than," "is greater than," or "equals."

9. 47 _____ 74

10. 1,444 _____ 1,399

11. 919 _____ 919

12. 436 _____ 4,360

13. 426 and 264 have the same digits, but in a different order. Do they have the same value? Explain.

_____

_____

14. Can you compare the 4 in 934 with the 4 in 647 to find how 934 and 647 compare? Explain.

_____

_____

Complete.

15. To compare 2,457 and 2,464 you should look at the

digits in the _____ place.

16. To compare 1,830 and 1,799 you should look at the

digits in the _____ place.

Ordering Numbers

Order from least to greatest.

1. 649, 469, 964 _____

2. 215, 512, 255 _____

3. 375, 752, 527 _____

4. 823, 838, 282 _____

5. 439, 394, 934 _____

Order from greatest to least.

6. 315, 153, 453 _____

7. 8,042; 4,028; 2,408 _____

8. 3,962; 2,396; 9,632 _____

9. 484, 884, 448 _____

10. 1,256; 1,652; 2,165 _____

11. Circle the number that comes between 3,010 and 3,325.

   3,001   3,332   3,125   3,521

12. Circle the greatest number.

   2,909   2,999   2,990   2,900

13. Write a number between 2,458 and 3,002.

   _____

14. Write a number between 2,999 and 3,008.

   _____

Rounding to Tens

Round to the nearest ten.

1. 47 _____

2. 14 _____

3. 25 _____

4. 42 _____

5. 38 _____

6. 16 _____

7. 111 _____

8. 105 _____

9. 674 _____

10. 417 _____

11. 326 _____

12. 575 _____

13. 233 _____

14. 620 _____

15. 337 _____

16. 517 _____

17. 224 _____

18. 889 _____

19. 28 _____

20. 620 _____

21. 55 _____

22. 155 _____

23. 8 _____

24. 404 _____

25. Joanne's bus was 27 minutes late tonight. She called to say she would be about a half hour late for dinner. Explain why this was correct.

_____

26. The library in Frank's town is 16 blocks from his house. When he asked to walk there alone, he told his mother that it was about 10 blocks away. Is this correct? Explain.

_____

27. Beth has read 218 pages of her new book. She tells a friend that to the nearest 10 she has read 210 pages. Is this correct?

_____

28. Name 3 two-digit numbers that round to 60 when rounded to the nearest ten.

_____

29. Name 3 three-digit numbers that round to 250 when rounded to the nearest ten.

_____

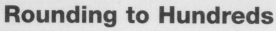

Rounding to Hundreds

Round to the nearest hundred.

1. 427 _____   **2.** 453 _____   **3.** $178 _____

4. 211 _____   **5.** $319 _____   **6.** 296 _____

7. 871 _____   **8.** $531 _____   **9.** 497 _____

10. 902 _____   **11.** 890 _____   **12.** 711 _____

13. 623 _____   **14.** 451 _____   **15.** 366 _____

16. $350 _____   **17.** 95 _____   **18.** $329 _____

19. Round 79 to the nearest hundred. _____

20. Round 152 to the nearest hundred. _____

21. Round 242 to the nearest hundred. _____

22. What is the greatest number that rounds to 700 when you round to the nearest hundred? _____

23. What is the least number that rounds to 700 when you round to the nearest hundred? _____

24. Write any 5 numbers less than 400 that round to 400 when you round to the nearest hundred.

_____

25. Write any 5 numbers greater than 400 that round to 400 when you round to the nearest hundred.

_____

26. Give the greatest and least numbers that round to 500 when rounded to the nearest 100.

_____

Name _____

Review and Practice

Vocabulary Match each with its definition.

_____ **1.** compare   **a.** one way to estimate

_____ **2.** round   **b.** to place a set of numbers from least
                                  to greatest or greatest to least

_____ **3.** order   **c.** a way to decide which of two
                                  numbers is greater

(Lesson 6) Compare. Use $<$, $>$, or $=$.

4. 623 $\bigcirc$ 632   **5.** 2,300 $\bigcirc$ 320   **6.** 556 $\bigcirc$ 655

7. 8,900 $\bigcirc$ 8,900   **8.** 367 $\bigcirc$ 1,240   **9.** 459 $\bigcirc$ 459

(Lesson 7) Order from least to greatest.

10. 308, 299, 315 _____

11. 2,453; 2,053; 998 _____

12. 1,245; 1,425; 542 _____

Order from greatest to least.

13. 5,180; 5,108; 5,810 _____

14. 606; 6,006; 6,600 _____

(Lesson 8) Round to the nearest ten.

15. 71 _____   **16.** 38 _____   **17.** $45 _____

(Lesson 9) Round to the nearest hundred.

18. 651 _____   **19.** $439 _____   **20.** $860 _____

21. Clara found pictures of her mother dated 1978, 1971,
1983, and 1973. Clara wants to put them in order from

oldest to newest. Write the dates in order. _____

(Mixed Review) Compare. Write $<$, $>$, or $=$.

22. 6 + 9 $\bigcirc$ 9 + 6   **23.** 8 − 5 $\bigcirc$ 7 − 2   **24.** 9 + 3 $\bigcirc$ 15 − 4

Time to the Nearest Five Minutes

Write each time two ways.

1.

_____

_____

2.

_____

_____

3.

_____

_____

4.

_____

_____

5.

_____

_____

6.

_____

_____

7. How many minutes are between 8:20 and 8:35? _____

8. What's another way to write 10 minutes before five? _____

9. Suppose it's 8:45. What time will it be
15 minutes later? _____

Exploring Time to the Nearest Minute

Write each time two ways.

1.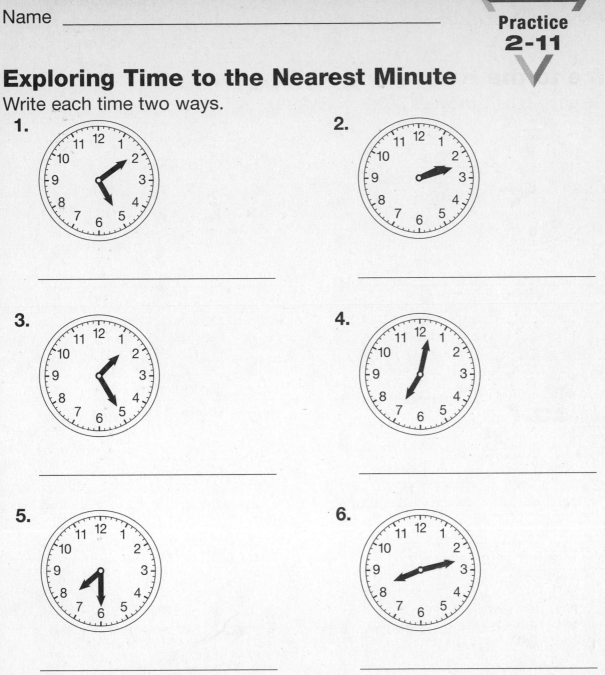

_____

2.

_____

3.

_____

4.

_____

5.

_____

6.

_____

7. Duke's vet appointment is at 4:30. You arrive at 4:17. Are you early or late?

_____

8. If it is 3:22, in how many minutes will it be 3:30?

_____

9. Suppose you waited 12 minutes for your school bus. About how many minutes did you wait? Round to the nearest ten minutes.

_____

Name _____

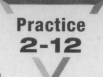
Time to the Half Hour and Quarter Hour

Write each time two ways. Write A.M. or P.M.

1.
go to a Saturday afternoon movie

_____

_____

2.
sunrise

_____

_____

3.
school's out

_____

_____

4.
sleep time

_____

_____

5.
dinner time

_____

_____

6.
lunch time

_____

_____

7. Write a time that is between noon and half past twelve in the afternoon. _____

8. Write a time that is between quarter to three and quarter after three in the morning. _____

9. How many times in one day will the clock show 6:30? Explain. _____

Elapsed Time

1. Sam wants to let his dog run for twenty minutes. If he starts at 12:15 P.M., what time should he call the dog in?

_____

2. "I tried to call you an hour ago!" says Sheila. If it is 8:45 P.M. now, what time did she call before?

_____

3. "This movie lasts for 2 hours and 45 minutes," says Marc. If it begins at 7:00 P.M., what time will the movie end?

_____

4. Kai started his homework at 4:35 P.M. and finished at 7:00 P.M. How much time did he spend doing homework?

_____

5. Carla's karate class lasts for 45 minutes. If it begins at 4:15 P.M., what time will it end?

_____

6. Suppose it is 6:20 A.M. What time will it be in half an hour?

_____

7. The school bus arrives at 7:15 A.M. It is now 6:35 A.M. How much time does Amir have to get ready?

_____

Three cars left school at 2:30 P.M. Each traveled for the amount of time shown. When did each car arrive at its destination?

Car	Driving Time	Arrival Time
8. Juan's car	35 minutes	_____
9. Hannah's car	60 minutes	_____
10. Beryl's car	1 hour and 5 minutes	_____

Name _____

Ordinal Numbers and the Calendar

Use the calendar to answer **1–6**.

February

Sun.	Mon.	Tues.	Wed.	Thur.	Fri.	Sat.
				1	2	3
4	5	6	7	8	9	10
11	12	13	14	15	16	17
18	19	20	21	22	23	24
25	26	27	28			

1. How many Tuesdays are in this month? _____

2. Abraham Lincoln was born on February 12th.

What day of the week is that? _____

Mark it on the calendar above.

3. George Washington was born on the twenty-second of February.

What day of the week is that? _____

Mark it on the calendar above.

4. What day of the week is February 3rd? _____

5. What is the date of the third Saturday in February?

_____

6. What are the dates of the last weekend in February?

_____

7. February is the second month of the year. What is the first month?

_____

8. Name the fourth month. _____

Decision Making

1. Part of making a schedule is knowing how much time
you have to get everything done. Figure out how much
time you have available for each activity on this list and
write it down.

Activity	Total time
a. The meeting begins at 3:15 P.M. and lasts until 4:00 P.M.	_____
b. You have from 6:00 P.M. until 8:20 P.M. to do your homework.	_____
c. Practice begins at 3:45 P.M. and ends at 5:15 P.M.	_____
d. You begin your chores at 8:30 A.M. and must be done by noon.	_____

2. Another step in making a schedule is estimating—or
guessing—how long something will take. Give it a try.
Estimate how long it would take you to:

a. brush your teeth _____

b. clean your room _____

c. read 10 pages _____

d. play a game of checkers _____

e. walk to the nearest store _____

f. make a sandwich _____

g. change your clothes _____

h. take a bath _____

Name _____

Review and Practice

Vocabulary Match each word with its definition.

_____ **1.** A.M.   **a.** times from noon to midnight

_____ **2.** P.M.   **b.** numbers used for ordering

_____ **3.** ordinal numbers   **c.** times from midnight to noon

(Lessons 10, 11, and 12) Write each time two ways. Write A.M. or P.M.

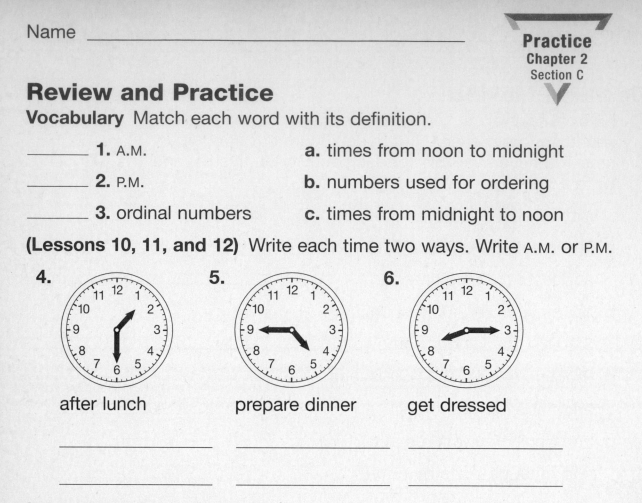

4. after lunch

5. prepare dinner

6. get dressed

_____   _____   _____

_____   _____

(Lesson 13) Write each time.

7. Daniela ate lunch at 12:30 P.M. and went fishing 2 hours and
15 minutes later. What time did she go fishing? _____

8. Justin began his chores at 9 A.M. and ended at 11:15 A.M. How long
was he doing his chores? _____

(Lesson 14) Use the calendar to answer **9** and **10.**

9. What day of the week
is the 23rd?

_____

10. How many Mondays are
in the month shown?

_____

October

Sun.	Mon.	Tues.	Wed.	Thur.	Fri.	Sat.
				1	2	3
4	5	6	7	8	9	10
11	12	13	14	15	16	17
18	19	20	21	22	23	24
25	26	27	28	29	30	31

(Mixed Review) Write the value of each digit in 473,826.

11. 8 _____   **12.** 4 _____

13. 7 _____

Cumulative Review

(Chapter 1 Lesson 2) Use the data from the graph to answer each question.

1. How many sports are the favorite of more than 5 students? _____

Students' Favorite Sports

Hockey
Basketball
Baseball
Tennis

0 1 2 3 4 5 6 7 8 9 10
Number of Students

2. What sport is the favorite of 9 students? _____

(Chapter 1 Lesson 5) Write a number sentence and use it to solve the problem.

3. Liz read 10 books. 6 were mysteries. The rest were biographies. How many were biographies? _____

(Chapter 1 Lesson 11) Write the next four numbers.

4. 10, 20, 30, 40, _____, _____, _____, _____

5. 29, 26, 23, 20, _____, _____, _____, _____

(Chapter 2 Lesson 4) Write the value of each underlined digit.

6. 645,861 _____   **7.** 293,862 _____

(Chapter 2 Lesson 7) Order from least to greatest.

8. 455, 450, 530, 545 _____

9. 4,670, 5,839, 4,668, 5,355 _____

(Chapter 2 Lesson 10) Write each time in two ways.

10.

11.

_____   _____

Exploring Addition Patterns

Use basic facts and place value to complete each problem.

1. 3 + 4 = _____

2. 30 + 40 = _____ tens + _____ tens

= _____ tens = _____

3. 300 + 400 = _____ hundreds + _____ hundreds

= _____ hundreds = _____

4. 3 + 5 = _____

30 + _____ = 80

_____ + 500 = 800

5. 4 + 9 = _____

_____ + 90 = 130

400 + _____ = 1,300

6. 8 + 1 = _____

80 + _____ = 90

_____ + 100 = 900

7. 8 + 7 = _____

_____ + 70 = 150

800 + _____ = 1,500

Find each sum using mental math.

8. $20 + $50 = _____

9. 100 + 700 = _____

10. 600 + 400 = _____

11. $30 + $80 = _____

12. 20 + 90 = _____

13. $60 + $70 = _____

14. There are 30 students on one school bus and 70 on another school bus. How many students are there altogether? _____

15. Can you use the basic fact 3 + 2 to add 30 + 200? Explain.

_____

_____

Name _____

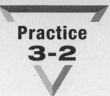
Exploring Adding on a Hundred Chart

You can think about adding numbers in different ways.

1. 50 + 36 = 50 + 30 + _____ = _____

Show how you can use the hundred chart to add 48 and 37.

2. 48 + 37 = _____

1	2	3	4	5	6	7	8	9	10
11	12	13	14	15	16	17	18	19	20
21	22	23	24	25	26	27	28	29	30
31	32	33	34	35	36	37	38	39	40
41	42	43	44	45	46	47	48	49	50
51	52	53	54	55	56	57	58	59	60
61	62	63	64	65	66	67	68	69	70
71	72	73	74	75	76	77	78	79	80
81	82	83	84	85	86	87	88	89	90
91	92	93	94	95	96	97	98	99	100

Find each sum. You may use the hundred chart to help.

3. 43 + 20 = _____   **4.** 52 + 18 = _____

5. 27 + 6 = _____   **6.** 6 + 27 = _____

7. $78 + $21 = _____   **8.** 40 + 45 = _____

9. 37 + 14 = _____   **10.** $13 + $29 = _____

11. Find the sum of 14 and 67. _____

12. Add 54 and 39. _____

13. If you know the sum of 24 + 37, how can you find the
sum of 37 + 24? Explain.

_____

_____

14. Explain how you would add 39 + 22 using mental math.

_____

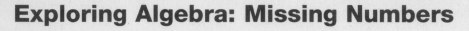

Exploring Algebra: Missing Numbers

There are two ways to find the missing

number in $\boxed{}$ + 4 = 21.

1. Match 4 cubes on one side with
4 on the other. How many more
cubes do you need to make 21?

_____ + 4 = 21.

2. You already have 4 on one side,
so you can count on from 4 until
you have 21.

You count on _____ more cubes.

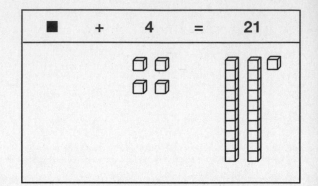

Find each missing number. You may use color cubes to help.

3. _____ + 7 = 23   **4.** _____ + 8 = 14   **5.** _____ + 5 = 12

6. _____ + 6 = 21   **7.** 4 + _____ = 10   **8.** 9 + _____ = 28

9. 11 + _____ = 19   **10.** _____ + 13 = 22   **11.** _____ + 19 = 23

12. Is the missing number in $\boxed{}$ + 4 = 16 the same as

the missing number in 4 + $\boxed{}$ = 16? Explain.

_____

_____

Use patterns to find each missing number.

13. _____ + 7 = 13   **14.** 6 + _____ = 13   **15.** _____ + 5 = 11

16. 6 + _____ = 11   **17.** 3 + _____ = 12   **18.** _____ + 9 = 12

Estimating Sums

Estimate each sum.

1. 48 + 39 _____

2. 713 + 224 _____

3. $354 + $239 _____

4. $77 + $62 _____

5. 85 + 41 _____

6. 528 + 867 _____

7. 91 + 26 _____

8. 333 + 690 _____

9. Estimate the sum of 915 and 166. _____

10. Estimate the sum of 43 and 25. _____

11. Estimate the sum of $67 and $62. _____

12. Two addends have a sum of about 800. What are two possible addends?

_____

13. Two addends have a sum of about 70. What are two possible addends?

_____

14. Round to find which two pairs of numbers have a sum of about 700.

412   355   268   508   149

_____

15. Round to estimate the sum of all the numbers in **14.**

_____

Review and Practice

Vocabulary Match each with its definition.

_____ 1. estimate

    a. the answer obtained when adding numbers

_____ 2. sum

    b. to find an answer that is close to an exact answer

(Lesson 1) Complete.

3. $8 + 8 =$ _____

    $80 +$ _____ $= 160$

    _____ $+ 800 = 1,600$

4. $\$3 + \$$_____ $= \$12$

    $\$$_____ $+ \$90 = \$120$

    $\$300 + \$900 = \$$_____

5. What basic fact can you use to find $300 + 800$? _____

(Lesson 2) Find each sum. You may use a hundred chart to help.

6. $36 + 8 =$ _____

7. $82 + 12 =$ _____

8. $25 + 30 =$ _____

9. $\$64 + \$27 =$ _____

(Lesson 3) Find each missing number. You may use color cubes to help.

10. _____ $+ 7 = 32$

11. $8 +$ _____ $= 30$

12. I am a 2-digit number. If you add me to 6 you will get a sum of 38. What number am I? _____

(Lesson 4) Circle the letter that shows the best estimate of each sum.

13. $34 + 55$ **a.** 80   **b.** 100   **c.** 90

14. $522 + 131$ **a.** 600   **b.** 700   **c.** 800

(Mixed Review) Use the pictograph to answer each question.

15. How many students does each 🐱 represent? _____

16. How many boys have cats? _____

17. How many more girls than boys have cats? _____

Cats Owned

girls 🐱 🐱 🐱 🐱 🐱

boys 🐱 🐱 🐱 🐱

Key: 1 🐱 = 3 students

Exploring Adding with Regrouping

Find each sum. You may use place-value blocks to help.

1. 24 + 47

    a. How many ones? _____

    b. Do you need to regroup? _____

    c. How many tens? _____

    d. Do you need to regroup? _____

    e. 24 + 47 = _____

2. 18 + 55 = _____

3. 34 + 28 = _____

4. 62 + 43 = _____

5. 59 + 21 = _____

6. 77 + 69 = _____

7. 45 + 86 = _____

8. 32 + 39 = _____

9. 29 + 99 = _____

10. 33 + 57 = _____

11. 62 + 39 = _____

12. 58 + 46 = _____

13. 16 + 86 = _____

14. 89 + 75 = _____

15. 57 + 24 = _____

16. 35 + 97 = _____

17. 59 + 79 = _____

18. Do you need to regroup 10 ones for 1 ten when you add 56 + 37?
Explain.

_____

19. Do you need to regroup 10 ones for 1 ten when you add
56 + 42? Explain.

_____

Adding 2-Digit Numbers

Add. Estimate to check.

1. 43
    + 16

2. 26
    + 72

3. $39
    + 41

4. 52
    + 9

5. 85
    + 67

6. 64
    + 89

7. 96
    + 6

8. $58
    + 15

9. 22
    + 81

10. $54
    + 7

11. 88
    + 99

12. 16
    + 77

13. 91
    + 79

14. 76
    + 37

15. 55
    + 86

16. 47
    + 65

17. 28 + 54 = _____

18. $37 + $78 = _____

19. 63 + 87 = _____

20. 92 + 21 = _____

21. Find the sum of 45 and 37. _____

22. Add 38 and 19. _____

23. Write two numbers that add to 70 without regrouping.

_____

24. When you add 27 + 5 do you start by adding 2 + 5? Explain.

_____

Adding 3-Digit Numbers

Complete.

1. $\overset{1\ 1}{2}17$
    $+\ 384$
    $\boxed{}01$

2. $58\overset{1}{3}$
    $+\ \ 74$
    $6\boxed{}\boxed{}$

3. $\$3\overset{1\ 1}{5}7$
    $+\ \ \ 66$
    $\boxed{}2\boxed{}$

4. $44\overset{1}{5}$
    $+\ 208$
    $\boxed{}\boxed{}\boxed{}$

Add. Estimate to check.

5. $\$826$
    $+\ \ 151$

6. 737
    $+217$

7. $\$42$
    $+\ 59$

8. 431
    $+\ 94$

9. 621
    $+377$

10. 456
    $+255$

11. 388
    $+\ 94$

12. $\$982$
    $+\ 635$

13. $97 + 42 =$ _____

14. $358 + 715 =$ _____

15. $\$39 + \$75 =$ _____

16. $118 + 647 =$ _____

17. Find the sum of 380 and 442.

_____

18. Find the sum of 832 and 79.

_____

19. Write two addends with a sum of 258.

_____

20. Estimate to decide which sum is greater than 1,000:
    $590 + 462$ or $311 + 628$.

_____

_____

Name _____

Adding 4-Digit Numbers:
Choose a Calculation Method

Add.

1. 5,347
   +2,491

2. 6,200
   +3,500

3. 4,619
   +1,592

4. 7,416
   +2,347

5. $2,400
   +5,500

6. 1,348
   + 721

7. 4,827
   +3,164

8. 6,038
   + 831

9. 6,371
   +2,293

10. 3,849
    +5,163

11. 7,345
    +1,681

12. 4,691
    +5,366

13. 1,495 + 5,622 = _____

14. 6,400 + 3,500 = _____

15. 9,046 + 716 = _____

16. $5,807 + $2,164 = _____

17. Find the sum of 648 and 2,115.

_____

18. Find the sum of 2,800 and 5,000.

_____

19. Estimate to decide if the sum of 6,701 and 2,399 is greater than or less than 10,000.

_____

_____

20. Which two numbers have a sum of 6,000?

| 1,500 | 5,000 | 3,000 |
| 2,000 | 4,500 | 3,500 |

_____

Name _____

Column Addition

Add.

1.
```
   78
   94
+   5
```

2.
```
   416
   172
+   21
```

3.
```
   660
   218
+   34
```

4.
```
    54
   793
 +415
```

5.
```
   348
   506
 +270
```

6.
```
   529
    32
 +410
```

7.
```
   481
     9
 +573
```

8.
```
   855
    26
 +  91
```

9. 84 + 394 + 250 = _____

10. 15 + 7 + 989 = _____

11. What is the sum of 23, 462, and 117?

12. Add 851, 756, and 922.

_____   _____

13. What is the greatest possible sum using three of these numbers?

| 97 | 541 | 472 | 149 | 608 |

_____

14. To add 67 + 45 + 821, would you start by adding 6 + 4 + 2? Why or why not?

_____

_____

15. Does it matter in which order you write 549, 192, 420 and 37 to add?

_____

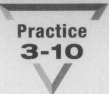
Analyze Strategies: Guess and Check

Guess and check to solve.

1. The Hawks beat the Jays in a baseball game. The scores were 6 runs apart and there were 22 runs scored in the game. How many runs did each team score?

   _____

2. The Hawks lost to the Orioles by 4 runs. There were 18 runs scored in the game. How many runs did the Orioles score?

   _____

Use any strategy to solve.

3. The Jays beat the Orioles by 8 runs. There were 16 runs scored in the game. How many runs did the Jays score?

   _____

4. The sum of two numbers is 65. The numbers are 3 apart. What are they?

   _____

5. The sum of two numbers is 92. The numbers are 12 apart. What are they?

   _____

6. Tim bought three items at the school bookstore. He spent $23. What did Tim buy? Use the prices in the table to solve.

Item	Cost
Backpack	$14
Calculator	$ 9
Dictionary	$ 5
Notebook	$ 3
Set of Markers	$ 4

   _____

   _____

Name _____

Review and Practice

(Lesson 5) Find each sum. You may use place-value blocks to help.

1. 68 + 35 = _____   **2.** 237 + 125 = _____

3. 56 + 39 = _____   **4.** 53 + 34 = _____

(Lessons 6 and 7) Add. Estimate to check.

5.   43   **6.**   651   **7.**   738   **8.**   49
   +24   + 86   +339   +71

9. 823 + 119 = _____   **10.** 545 + 126 = _____

11. Do you need to regroup 10 tens for 1 hundred when you
add 241 + 387? _____

(Lessons 8 and 9) Add.

12. 2,568   **13.**   355   **14.**   402   **15.** 7,220
  + 812   51   313   + 867
            + 19   + 66

(Lesson 10) Guess and check to solve.

16. The Jays beat the Tigers by 5 runs. There were 17 runs
scored. How many runs did the Jays score? _____

(Mixed Review) Circle the letter that answers each question.

17. Which does not tell the correct time?

   A. half after 5   **B.** 15 minutes before 5

   C. 4:45   **D.** 45 minutes after 4

18. What time will it be in 1 and a half hours?

   A. 4:15   **B.** 6:00   **C.** 6:15   **D.** 7:30

19. Sal's soccer practice began at 2:45 P.M. and finished at
4:00 P.M. How long was practice?

_____

Name _____

Mental Math

Use mental math to find each sum.

1. 80 + 55 = _____   2. 62 + 9 = _____

3. 18 + 40 = _____   4. 45 + 35 = _____

5. 59 + 36 = _____   6. 21 + 18 = _____

7. 99 + 5 = _____   8. 73 + 9 = _____

9. 47 + 29 = _____   10. 25 + 60 = _____

11. 88 + 4 = _____   12. 7 + 43 = _____

13. 81 + 9 = _____   14. 27 + 62 = _____

15. 7 + 19 = _____   16. 32 + 21 = _____

17. 55 + 35 = _____   18. 28 + 83 = _____

19. 46 + 52 = _____   20. 67 + 9 = _____

21. 34 + 28 = _____   22. 35 + 17 = _____

23. 8 + 37 = _____   24. 42 + 17 = _____

25. Find the sum of 475 and 15.   26. Find the sum of 133 and 7.

_____   _____

27. Add 389 + 4.   28. Add 225 + 25.

_____   _____

29. How does knowing 7 + 3 = 10 help you to add 37 + 13 mentally?

_____

_____

30. How can finding digits that add up to 10 help you to add 64 + 26?

_____

_____

Name _____

Counting Coins

Write the total value in cents.

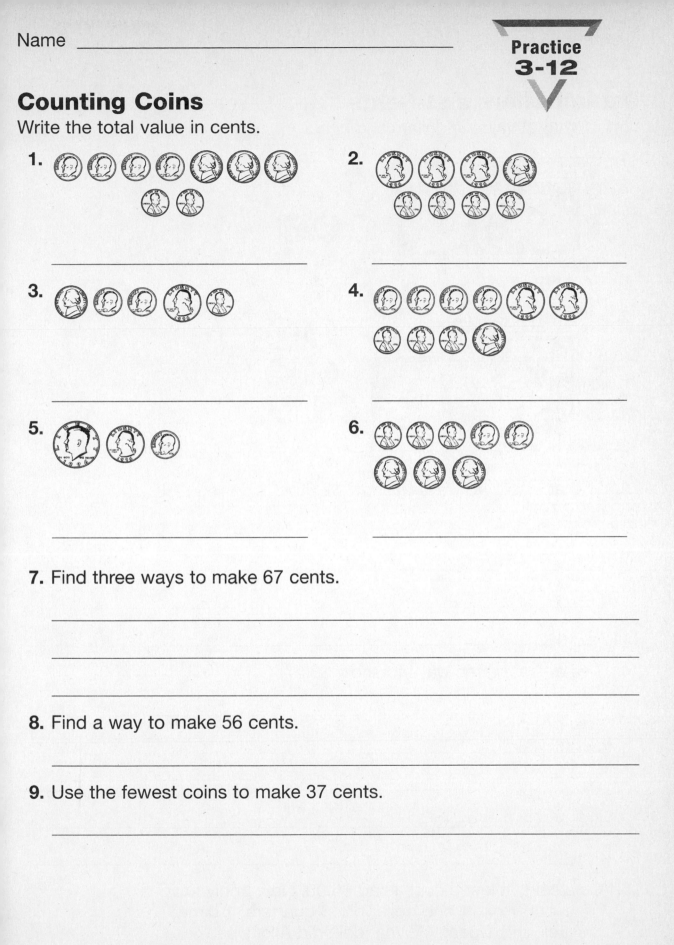

1.

2.

_____

_____

3.

4.

_____

_____

5.

6.

_____

_____

7. Find three ways to make 67 cents.

_____

_____

_____

8. Find a way to make 56 cents.

_____

9. Use the fewest coins to make 37 cents.

_____

Name _____

Using Dollars and Cents

Write the total value in dollars and cents.

1.

_____

2.

_____

3. Give at least two ways to show $2.65.

_____

_____

_____

_____

4. Give at least three ways to show $8.57.

_____

_____

_____

_____

_____

5. Alicia said, "I lost a coin! I had $6.96. Now I only have
1 five-dollar bill, 1 one-dollar bill, 3 quarters, 1 dime,
1 nickel, and 1 penny." What coin did Alicia lose?

_____

Name _____

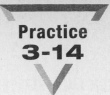
Exploring Making Change

Your class is having an art sale to make money for new
supplies. You are the cashier.

1. Andy buys a papier-maché mask worth $3.24. He pays with $5.00.
How much change will you give him?

    a. Count on by circling the coins and bills you will use to make
    change. Write the amount.

    _____ _____ _____ _____

    b. How much change is that? _____

2. June buys a painting worth $3.31. She pays with $5.00. List which
coins and bills you would use to make change. Then write the change
in dollars and cents.

_____

_____

3. Sheila's purchases total $2.09. She pays with $3.00.

    a. Write three ways you could make change.

    _____

    _____

    _____

    b. Which way uses the fewest coins?

    _____

Adding Money

Add. Estimate to check.

1. $5.17
   + 4.39

2. $8.89
   + 3.14

3. $0.52
   + 7.93

4. $2.22
   + 3.33

5. $4.87
   + 5.14

6. $2.06
   + 7.34

7. $9.40
   + 1.61

8. $6.73
   + 2.99

9. $4.34 + $3.71 = _____

10. $9.49 + $8.84 = _____

11. $3.25 + $2.96 = _____

12. $7.69 + $5.91 = _____

13. Find the sum of $2.41 and $5.57. _____

14. Add $8.12 + $8.69. _____

15. Will $10.00 be enough to buy a
softball and a baseball bat? Explain.

_____

16. Which two pieces of equipment together
will cost about $11.00?

Athletic Equipment	
baseball bat	$7.07
basketball	$6.49
volleyball	$3.34
softball	$2.98
soccer ball	$4.83

_____

17. What two items together would cost
less than $7.00? How much would they cost?

_____

Name _____

Front-End Estimation

Use front-end estimation to estimate each sum.

1. $6.12
+ 3.77

2. 334
865
+202

3. 789
122
+960

4. $2.57
5.16
+ 8.45

5. 691
423
+606

6. 928
+890

7. $3.33
5.87
+ 6.63

8. 478
150
+822

9. 345 + 312 + 637 _____

10. 841 + 797 + 141 _____

11. Use front-end estimation to estimate the sum of 263, 804, and 469.

_____

12. Use front-end estimation to estimate the sum of $7.34, $3.69, and $9.51.

_____

13. Is the sum of $4.32 + $6.90 + $7.86 greater than $17.00? Explain.

_____

14. If you buy 2 items that cost $6.32 each, will $11.00 be enough to buy both items? Explain.

_____

15. If you buy 3 items that cost $5.43 each, will $15.00 be enough to buy all 3 items? Explain.

_____

16. If you buy 2 items for $6.29 and 1 item for $3.55, will $15.00 be enough? Explain.

_____

Name _____

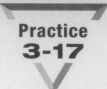

Analyze Word Problems: Exact Answer or Estimate?

Ahmed is going shopping for art supplies.

Art Supplies	
crayons	$2.34
marker	$4.98
paintbrush	$1.86
construction paper	$3.15
watercolor paint set	$4.43
frame	$6.71

Write if you need an exact answer or an estimate. Then solve.

1. Ahmed has a $10 bill. Does he have enough money to buy construction paper and a frame? Explain.

_____

2. How much would it cost to buy crayons, a marker, and construction paper?

_____

3. If Ahmed has $8.00, and he buys 3 paint brushes, does he have enough money left to buy a watercolor paint set? Explain.

_____

_____

_____

4. Ahmed wants to know if $9.00 is enough to buy 2 markers. Does he need to find the exact total? Explain.

_____

5. Ahmed began shopping at 11:30 A.M. When he finished it was 12:15 P.M. How long did he spend shopping?

_____

Name _____

Review and Practice

(Lesson 11) Use mental math to find each sum.

1. 75 + 9 _____   **2.** 29 + 43 _____   **3.** 88 + 5 _____

(Lessons 12 and 13) Write the total value in cents or dollars and cents.

4. _____

5. _____

(Lesson 14) List which coins and bills you would use to make change. Then write the change in dollars and cents.

6. Metta buys a notebook that costs $1.19. She pays with $2.00.

_____

(Lesson 15) Add. Estimate to check.

7. $9.15 + $4.82 _____   **8.** $3.56 + $6.89 _____

9. $1.75 + $9.10 _____   **10.** $7.29 + $0.54 _____

(Lesson 16) Use front-end estimation to estimate each sum.

11. 325 + 176 + 852 _____   **12.** 63 + 55 + 38 _____

(Lesson 17) Write if you need an exact answer or an estimate. Then solve.

13. Cheryl wants to buy three books that cost $5.95, $2.95, and $3.45. Will $10 be enough money? Explain.

_____

_____

(Mixed Review) Write the value of each underlined number.

14. 4̲5,886 _____   **15.** 2,84̲6 _____   **16.** 1̲23,654 _____

Cumulative Review
(Chapter 1, Lesson 1)

1. Which of the following uses pictures to represent information in a graph?

   A. line graph   **B.** bar graph   **C.** pictograph

   _____

(Chapter 1, Lesson 3)

2. Which of the following shows changes over time?

   A. line graph   **B.** bar graph   **C.** pictograph

   _____

(Chapter 2, Lesson 4) Write the standard form of each number.

3. four hundred thousand, sixty-seven _____

4. six hundred twenty-one thousand, one hundred ten _____

5. one hundred thirty thousand, six _____

(Chapter 2, Lesson 9) Round each to the nearest hundred.

6. 2,610   7. 987   8. 1,651   9. 705

_____   _____   _____   _____

(Chapter 3, Lessons 9 and 15) Add.

10. $\begin{array}{r} 456 \\ 238 \\ +115 \\ \hline \end{array}$
11. $\begin{array}{r} 321 \\ 56 \\ +135 \\ \hline \end{array}$
12. $\begin{array}{r} \$3.15 \\ +1.49 \\ \hline \end{array}$
13. $\begin{array}{r} \$5.11 \\ +7.52 \\ \hline \end{array}$

(Chapter 3, Lesson 12)

14. Dimitrios has a five-dollar bill, 2 one-dollar bills, 3 quarters, 1 dime and 2 nickels. How much money does he have?

   _____

Name _____

Reviewing the Meaning of Subtraction

Write a number sentence for each. Then solve.

1. A clown is juggling four bananas. He drops one of them. How many bananas are still in the air?

_____

2. Karen invites eight friends to her home for a party. Three people cannot come. How many people are there for the party?

_____

3. Josh had a spelling test today. There were fifteen questions on the test. Josh misspelled six words. How many did he spell correctly?

_____

4. Twelve children attended Melissa's party. There were seven boys. How many girls were there?

_____

5. The bus stops and six children get on. Now there are thirteen children on the bus. How many children were on the bus before this stop?

_____

6. The cracker box contained eighteen crackers. Now there are only nine. How many crackers were taken?

_____

7. Jennifer has read 4 chapters of her book. The book has 16 chapters. How many chapters does she have left to read?

_____

8. Phil has $10. He buys a vase for $6. How much money does he have left?

_____

Name _____

Exploring Subtraction Patterns

Complete.

1. $8 - 3 =$ _____

_____ $- 30 = 50$

$800 -$ _____ $= 500$

2. $13 -$ _____ $= 9$

$130 - 40 =$ _____

_____ $- 400 = 900$

3. $\$19 - \$7 =$ _____

$\$190 -$ _____ $= \$120$

_____ $- \$700 = \$1,200$

4. $12 - 6 =$ _____

_____ $- 60 = 60$

_____ $- 600 = 600$

Find each difference using mental math.

5. $90 - 50 =$ _____

7. $1,800 - 400 =$ _____

9. $1,700 - 500 =$ _____

6. $\$100 - \$80 =$ _____

8. $\$1,200 - \$1,100 =$ _____

10. $\$1,100 - \$600 =$ _____

11. Karima and Rick are playing a game with play money. Rick has $1,100. He lands on a space that makes him pay Karima $400. How much money will he have left? _____

12. Marty and Dee live in the same town. Marty's grandparents live 30 miles away. Dee's grandparents live 80 miles away. How much farther away do Dee's grandparents live? _____

13. Continue the pattern. Then write the rule.

In	70	80	90	100	110	120
Out	40	50	60			

Rule: _____

14. What basic fact could you use to find $1,300 - 500$? Solve.

_____

Exploring Subtracting on a Hundred Chart

Find each difference. You may use a hundred chart to help.

1. 92 − 27 = _____

2. 69 − 16 = _____

3. 29 − 12 = _____

4. $77 − $64 = _____

5. 44 − 11 = _____

6. 54 − 37 = _____

Use mental math to find each difference.

7. 71 − 51 = _____

8. $48 − $20 = _____

9. 80 − 40 = _____

10. $45 − $30 = _____

11. 42 − 22 = _____

12. 51 − 21 = _____

13. 31 − 8 = _____

14. 79 − 44 = _____

Find each missing number. You may use a hundred chart to help.

15. 56 − _____ = 21

16. 32 − _____ = 7

17. _____ − 12 = 49

18. _____ − 34 = 62

19. 88 − _____ = 71

20. 89 − _____ = 61

21. On a hundred chart, Lesley begins with her finger on 89. She moves back 5 rows and back 7 spaces.

  a. On what number does she land? _____

  b. What number did she subtract? _____

22. Victor has 40¢. He wants to buy 3 postcards. Each postcard costs 20¢. How much more money will he need to buy the postcards?

  _____

Name _____

Estimating Differences

Estimate each difference.

1. 988 − 112 = _____   **2.** 992 − 400 = _____

3. 25 − 14 = _____   **4.** 98 − 22 = _____

5. 112 − 56 = _____   **6.** 506 − 210 = _____

7. 279 − 126 = _____   **8.** 767 − 547 = _____

9. $4.99 − $3.67 = _____   **10.** $8.22 − $4.83 = _____

11. $6.49 − $1.25 = _____   **12.** $5.81 − $2.84 = _____

13. 432 − 121 = _____   **14.** 890 − 160 = _____

15. 62 − 19 = _____   **16.** 81 − 76 = _____

17. Suppose the length of a movie you plan to watch is
98 minutes. You have been watching it for 50 minutes.
Would it make sense to say that you have watched
about half of the movie? Explain.

_____

_____

18. Suppose the book that you're reading has 126 pages.
You've read 62 pages. Would it make sense to say that
you have read about half of the book? Explain.

_____

19. The estimated difference of the cost of two games is
$2.00. Give two examples of the exact amounts that
would make the estimate reasonable.

_____

_____

20. The estimated difference of the weight of two elephants
is 100 pounds. Give two examples of the exact amounts
that would make the estimate reasonable.

_____

Exploring Regrouping

Regroup 1 ten for 10 ones. You may use place-value blocks or draw a picture to help.

1. 64 is the same as _____

2. 42 = 3 tens, _____ ones

3. 95 = 8 tens, _____ ones

4. 63 = 5 tens, _____ ones

5. 57 = 4 tens, _____ ones

6. 53 = 4 tens, _____ ones

7. _____ = 5 tens, 17 ones

8. 32 = _____ tens, 12 ones

9. 90 = 8 tens, _____ ones

10. _____ = 3 tens, 11 ones

11. 88 = _____ tens, 18 ones

Regroup 1 hundred for 10 tens. You may use place-value blocks or draw a picture to help.

12. 215 = 1 hundred, _____ tens, 5 ones

13. 829 = 7 hundreds, _____ tens, 9 ones

14. 982 = 8 hundreds, _____ tens, 2 ones

15. 302 = 2 hundreds, _____ tens, 2 ones

16. 786 = 6 hundreds, _____ tens, 6 ones

17. 614 = 5 hundreds, _____ tens, 4 ones

18. Regroup 1 ten for 10 ones in the number 567.

_____

19. Regroup 1 hundred for 10 tens in the number 412.

_____

Review and Practice

(Lesson 1) Write a number sentence for each. Then solve.

1. Harold bought 5 souvenirs in Maine and 3 in Massachusetts. How many more souvenirs did he buy in Maine than Massachusetts? _____

2. Phylis took 18 pictures. 9 are of the Grand Canyon. How many pictures are not of the Grand Canyon? _____

(Lesson 2) Look for a pattern. Complete.

3. $6 - 2 =$ _____

   $60 -$ _____ $= 40$

   _____ $- 200 = 400$

4. $13 -$ _____ $= 4$

   $130 - 90 =$ _____

   _____ $- 900 = 400$

5. $17 - 8 =$ _____

   $170 -$ _____ $= 90$

   $1,700 - 800 =$ _____

(Lesson 3) Solve. You may use a hundred chart to help.

6. $35 - 5 =$ _____

7. $\$73 - \$30 =$ _____

8. $83 - 64 =$ _____

9. $59 - 17 =$ _____

10. _____ $- 45 = 55$

11. _____ $- 28 = 16$

(Lesson 4) Estimate each difference.

12. $623 - 455$ _____

13. $\$3.75 - \$2.29$ _____

14. Suppose a movie lasts 100 minutes. Does it make sense to say you have about 30 minutes of the show to watch when you've been watching for 47 minutes? Explain.

_____

(Lesson 5) Regroup 1 ten as 10 ones or 1 hundred as 10 tens. You may use place-value blocks or draw a picture to help.

15. 5 ☐☐

    5 ₆ 4

16. ☐☐ 2

    ₈ 8 2

17. ☐☐ 0

    ₄ 9 0

(Mixed Review) Find each sum.

18. $30 + 60 =$ _____

19. $400 + 300 =$ _____

20. $90 + 20 =$ _____

Exploring Subtracting 2-Digit Numbers

1. Find 86 − 48. You may use place-value blocks or draw a picture to help.

    a. Regroup 1 ten for 10 ones in the number 86.

        _____ tens and _____ ones.

    b. Subract the ones. _____ ones

    c. Subtract the tens. _____ tens

    d. The difference is _____.

Find each difference. You may use place-value blocks or draw a picture to help.

2. 28 − 17 = _____

3. 41 − 6 = _____

4. $97 − $16 = _____

5. 87 − 68 = _____

6. 33 − 25 = _____

7. $55 − $7 = _____

8. 19 − 11 = _____

9. 63 − 6 = _____

10. $77 − $48 = _____

11. 23 − 15 = _____

12. Subtract 23 from 81. _____

13. Find the difference of 63 and 47. _____

14. Find 91 − 52. _____

15. Your class needs to sell 50 tickets to the school show in order to win a prize. So far the class has sold 22 tickets. How many more tickets need to be sold? _____

16. Suppose you had a quarter, 2 dimes, and 7 pennies. If you lost 3 of your pennies, how much money would you have? _____

17. Genevieve has 60 minutes of homework to do. She has done 44 minutes. How many more minutes of homework does she have to do? _____

18. Yuki has read 14 pages of his 51-page book. How many more pages does he have left to read? _____

Subtracting 2-Digit Numbers

Subtract. Check each answer.

1. 76
    − 4 2

2. 6 3
    − 2 4

3. 3 4
    −   7

4. $5 5
    − 1 3

5. 8 2
    − 5 4

6. 2 9
    − 1 8

7. $2 1
    −   9

8. 7 0
    − 1 5

9. 3 2
    −   8

10. 9 7
     − 6 9

11. 6 0
     − 3 1

12. 4 2
     − 1 1

13. 37 − 28 = _____

14. 53 − 15 = _____

15. $24 − $6 = _____

16. 85 − 44 = _____

17. 66 − 39 = _____

18. 41 − 14 = _____

19. Find the difference of 50 and 18. _____

20. Subtract 27 from 42. _____

21. Write two numbers you could subtract from 25 with regrouping.

_____

22. Write two numbers you could subtract from 83 without regrouping.

_____

23. To subtract 22 from 74 do you need to regroup? Explain.

_____

Exploring Subtracting 3-Digit Numbers

Use place-value blocks to help you subtract.

Find 236 − 141.

1. Do you need to regroup to subtract the ones? Explain.

_____

2. Do you need to regroup to subtract the tens? Explain.

_____

3. Find the difference.　☐☐

```
  2 3 6
− 1 4 1
```

Find each difference. You may use place-value blocks or draw a picture to help.

4. 176 − 119 = _____　　**5.** 218 − 54 = _____

6. 343 − 161 = _____　　**7.** 135 − 72 = _____

8. 282 − 137 = _____　　**9.** 329 − 258 = _____

10. 191 − 78 = _____　　**11.** 245 − 195 = _____

12. Subtract 37 from 129. _____　　**13.** Subtract 274 from 388. _____

14. Suppose you had 193 baseball cards and your brother had 249. How many more does your brother have? _____

Subtracting 3-Digit Numbers
Subtract. Check each answer.

1.
```
  342
- 138
```

2.
```
  184
- 123
```

3.
```
  569
- 298
```

4.
```
  257
-  75
```

5.
```
  85
- 29
```

6.
```
  614
- 433
```

7.
```
  $232
-  225
```

8.
```
  94
- 38
```

9.
```
  427
- 164
```

10.
```
  $394
-  126
```

11.
```
  235
-  81
```

12.
```
  522
- 332
```

13. $154 - 119 =$ _____

14. $244 - 51 =$ _____

15. $363 - 147 =$ _____

16. $\$878 - \$56 =$ _____

17. $568 - 284 =$ _____

18. $216 - 162 =$ _____

19. Find the difference of 426 and 301. _____

20. Subtract 356 from 637. _____

21. Explain how to regroup to find $224 - 153$.

_____

_____

22. Kim says, "To subtract 164 from 573, I began by subtracting 3 ones from 4 ones." What did she do wrong?

_____

_____

Subtracting with 2 Regroupings

Subtract. Check each answer.

1. 346
   − 167
   ☐☐9

2. 182
   − 95
   ☐7

3. 225
   − 48
   1☐☐

4. 814
   − 526
   ☐8☐

5. 751
   − 383

6. 427
   − 148

7. $83
   − 59

8. 520
   − 451

9. 442
   − 86

10. 653
   − 275

11. 237
   − 179

12. 866
   − 77

13. 413 − 166 = _____

14. 243 − 59 = _____

15. $961 − $585 = _____

16. 92 − 36 = _____

17. 286 − 197 = _____

18. 354 − 188 = _____

19. Find the difference of 365 and 187. _____

20. Subtract 45 from 219. _____

21. Andrea subtracted 736 − 108 and found 628. She then added 736 and 108 to check her answer. Did she check her answer correctly? Explain.

_____

_____

22. To find 415 − 136, would you need to regroup hundreds? Explain.

_____

_____

Name _____

Subtracting Across 0

Subtract. Check each answer.

1. 207
   − 82

2. $403
   − 235

3. 800
   − 38

4. 520
   − 359

5. 309
   − 151

6. 705
   − 467

7. 631
   − 206

8. $104
   − 59

9. 240
   − 198

10. 501
    − 164

11. 408
    − 311

12. 202
    − 28

13. 306 − 147 = _____

14. 500 − 279 = _____

15. 940 − 458 = _____

16. 409 − 45 = _____

17. 604 − 335 = _____

18. 201 − 142 = _____

19. 703 − 497 = _____

20. 506 − 249 = _____

21. What is 703 minus 216? _____

22. Subtract 127 from 400. _____

23. Antonio said, "To solve 506 − 288, I can think of 5
hundreds as 50 tens." How might this help him subtract?

_____

_____

24. Write a number you could subtract from 202 without regrouping.

_____

Name _____

Review and Practice

(Lessons 7 and 9) Subtract. Check each answer.

1.	8 7	2.	5 6	3.	9 5	4.	7 3
	− 3 8		− 2 7		− 5 4		− 9

5. $371 - 369 =$ _____

6. $641 - 470 =$ _____

7. $974 - 58 =$ _____

8. $356 - 175 =$ _____

9. $342 - 159 =$ _____

10. $813 - 645 =$ _____

(Lessons 10 and 11) Subtract. Check each answer.

11.	$8 7 0	12.	5 5 6	13.	9 5 1	14.	7 0 3
	− 3 8 5		− 2 7 9		− 5 0 4		− 9 9

15. $871 - 119 =$ _____

16. $601 - 473 =$ _____

17. $900 - 58 =$ _____

18. $$306 - $177 =$ _____

19. $801 - 566 =$ _____

20. $709 - 23 =$ _____

21. Find the difference of 823 and 179. _____

22. Russia is 62 miles from Alaska. Washington is 500 miles from Alaska. How much farther from Alaska is Washington than Russia? _____

(Mixed Review) Write each time two ways.

23.	24.	25.

_____   _____   _____

_____   _____   _____

_____   _____   _____

Name _____

Subtracting 4-Digit Numbers:
Choose a Calculation Method

Solve. Check each answer.

1. 4,282
  − 1,718
	2. $6,359
	  − 3,342
		3. 3,200
		  − 2,000
			4. 7,650
			  − 5,365

5. 2,476
  − 1,684
	6. 5,699
	  − 3,940
		7. 9,100
		  − 4,500
			8. $4,375
			  − 3,350

9. 1,671
  − 400
	10. $6,500
	  − 999
		11. 3,124
		  − 1,482
			12. 8,146
			  −7,938

13. 5,442 − 2,200 = _____

14. $6,255 − $1,391 = _____

15. $1,450 − 650 = _____

16. 3,581 − 2,766 = _____

17. 4,733 − 3,627 = _____

18. 7,549 − 4,198 = _____

19. 5,555 − 3,472 = _____

20. 4,356 − 2,987 = _____

21. Subtract 1,234 from 4,321. _____

22. Subtract 6,487 from 7,486. _____

23. Subtract 8,322 from 9,323. _____

24. How could you use mental math to find 1,400 − 500?

_____

25. Leo subtracted 232 from 1,345 on his calculator and
found 113. Estimate to check. Is his answer reasonable?

_____

Analyze Word Problems: Multiple-Step Problems
Solve each problem.

Movie Admission Prices

Before 6 P.M.

Children under 12	$2
Adults	$5

After 6 P.M.

Children under 12	$3
Adults	$8

---

1. Mr. and Mrs. Riley want to take their 2 children to the movies. Their children are 5 and 9 years old.

   a. How much will it cost for them to see a movie before 6:00 P.M.? _____

   b. How much more will it cost for them to see a movie after 6:00 P.M.? _____

2. Mr. Ramirez told his 9-year old son that he could have $20 to take his friends to the movies. He wants to invite 4 friends from his class and his 14-year-old brother. How much more money does he need to take everyone to see a movie at 7:00 P.M.? _____

3. A scout troop leader is taking 14 scouts to the movies. Three scouts canceled and 5 more decided to go. How many scouts are going to the movies ? _____

4. The manager sold 55 adult tickets and 20 children's tickets for an afternoon movie. How many more adult tickets were sold than children's tickets? _____

Mental Math

Write what number you would add to each in order to subtract mentally.
Subtract.

1. 34 − 19 = _____

    I added _____.

2. 63 − 28 = _____

    I added _____.

3. 62 − 36 = _____

    I added _____.

4. 188 − 9 = _____

    I added _____.

5. 154 − 37 = _____

    I added _____.

6. 156 − 39 = _____

    I added _____.

7. 87 − 28 = _____

    I added _____.

8. 71 − 37 = _____

    I added _____.

9. 92 − 45 = _____

    I added _____.

10. 109 − 69 = _____

    I added _____.

11. 168 − 49 = _____

    I added _____.

12. 144 − 67 = _____

    I added _____.

13. What could you add to each number to find 730 − 260? Explain.

_____

_____

14. Would you add on to help you find 58 − 20? Explain.

_____

_____

Subtracting Money

Subtract.

1. $5.8 6
   –   2.5 5

2. $2 0.0 0
   –   7.0 5

3. $7.0 0
   –   5.7 6

4. $6.2 5
   –   2.9 8

5. $1 0.0 0
   –   5.8 7

6. $8.7 5
   –   4.3 5

7. $8.2 8
   –   4.9 9

8. $1 5.0 0
   –   3.8 9

9. $8.9 8
   –   2.7 9

10. $1 7.0 0
   –   6.7 2

11. $6.8 7
   –   1.9 8

12. $5.2 4
   –   4.2 5

13. $6.50 – $2.17 = _____

14. $11.50 – $6.75 = _____

15. $13.85 – $5.98 = _____

16. $20.00 – $8.88 = _____

17. $9.89 – $3.57 = _____

18. $15.00 – $7.99 = _____

19. Rachel bought a puzzle for $4.89. She gave the
clerk $10.00. How much change did she receive? _____

20. Diego bought a toy and paid with $5.00. He
received $3.29 in change. How much did the toy cost? _____

21. Sophie is buying toothpaste. Superclean costs
$4.89 and Sparkles cost $3.24. How much will
Sophie save if she buys Sparkles? _____

22. Sophie pays for Sparkles toothpaste with a $5 bill.
How much change will she receive? _____

Analyze Strategies: Use Objects

Use objects to help solve each problem.

1. Kendra is going to a hockey game at the arena. She climbs 2 steps at a time to get to the door faster. Her little brother climbs 1 step at a time.

   a. When Kendra has climbed 6 steps, how many steps has her brother taken? _____

   b. When Kendra has climbed 12 steps, how many steps has her brother taken? _____

2. Keith is waiting in line to buy snacks. There are 8 people ahead of him. Two people leave the line without buying anything. Four people buy their snacks and go to their seats. How many people are ahead of him now? _____

3. Doug counts the pennies in his piggy bank. His sister has two pennies for every one penny Doug has. Doug has 9 pennies. How many pennies does his sister have? _____

4. Sheila lives 3 times as far from the school as Julia. If it takes Julia 5 minutes to walk to school, how long will it take Sheila? _____

5. From school, Kathy walks 2 blocks, then 1 block to mail a letter. She walks on 4 more blocks toward home. How many blocks does she walk in all? _____

Use any strategy to help you solve this problem.

6. Shandra rode her bike 1 mile to school. It took her 15 minutes. How long should it take Shandra to ride her bike 3 miles to the bookstore? _____

Name _____

Review and Practice

(Lesson 12) Solve. Check each answer.

1.	5,7 3 8 − 2,6 6 7	**2.**	6,3 0 0 − 4,0 0 0	**3.**	7,8 5 6 − 2,1 3 3	**4.**	5,0 0 0 − 4,0 2 5

(Lesson 13) Solve.

5. It cost $3 for a child's ticket and $5 for an adult's ticket at the museum. Peter is going to the museum with his two sisters, Uncle Joe, and his mother. Peter and his 2 sisters can each get child's tickets. How much will it cost? _____

(Lesson 14) Write what number you would add to each in order to subtract mentally. Subtract.

6. $64 − 45 =$ _____   **7.** $372 − 68 =$ _____   **8.** $134 − 29 =$ _____

Add: _____   Add: _____   Add: _____

(Lesson 15) Subtract.

9.	$4.5 6 − 1.3 8	**10.**	$3.8 9 − 2.9 9	**11.**	$9.0 0 − 3.4 6	**12.**	$1 5.8 9 − 9.6 9

(Lesson 16) Use objects or any strategy to solve.

13. Tippy woke up at 7:00 A.M. She played for 1 hour. Then she napped. She woke up to play for another hour. Then she slept until Maggie came home from school at 3:00 P.M. How many hours did Tippy sleep? _____

(Mixed Review) Write each time.

14. Elizabeth did her homework at 4:30 P.M. and ate dinner 1 hour and 20 minutes later. What time did she eat? _____

15. Jerome got dressed for school at 7:15 A.M. Eight and a half hours later he returned home. What time was it when Jerome got home? _____

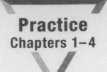
Cumulative Review
(Chapter 2 Lesson 13)

1. Brooke starts school at 8:10 A.M. School lets out
   at 3:25 P.M. How long is Brooke's school day? _____

   A. 8 hours

   B. 7 hours, 35 minutes

   C. 7 hours, 15 minutes

   D. 5 hours, 15 minutes

(Chapter 3 Lesson 14)

2. Clark bought a sandwich for a total of $2.35.
   He gave the sales person a $5 bill. What is
   the amount of change he should receive? _____

   A. $3, 6 dimes, and 1 nickel

   B. $2, 6 dimes, and 1 nickel

   C. $2, 5 dimes, and 5 pennies

(Chapter 3 Lesson 15)

3.	$2.19 + 1.97	4.	$3.05 + 1.50	5.	$6.89 + 3.27

6. Find the sum of $8.78 and $3.29. _____

7. What is the sum of $12.15 and $8.29? _____

   A. $10.44   **B.** $20.14   **C.** $20.44   **D.** not here

(Chapter 4 Lessons 7–9)

Find each difference.

8.	56 – 12	9.	27 – 9	10.	342 – 116	11.	2,892 – 1,451

12. Find the difference of 517 and 230. _____

13. Subtract 338 from 522. _____

Exploring Equal Groups

Complete.

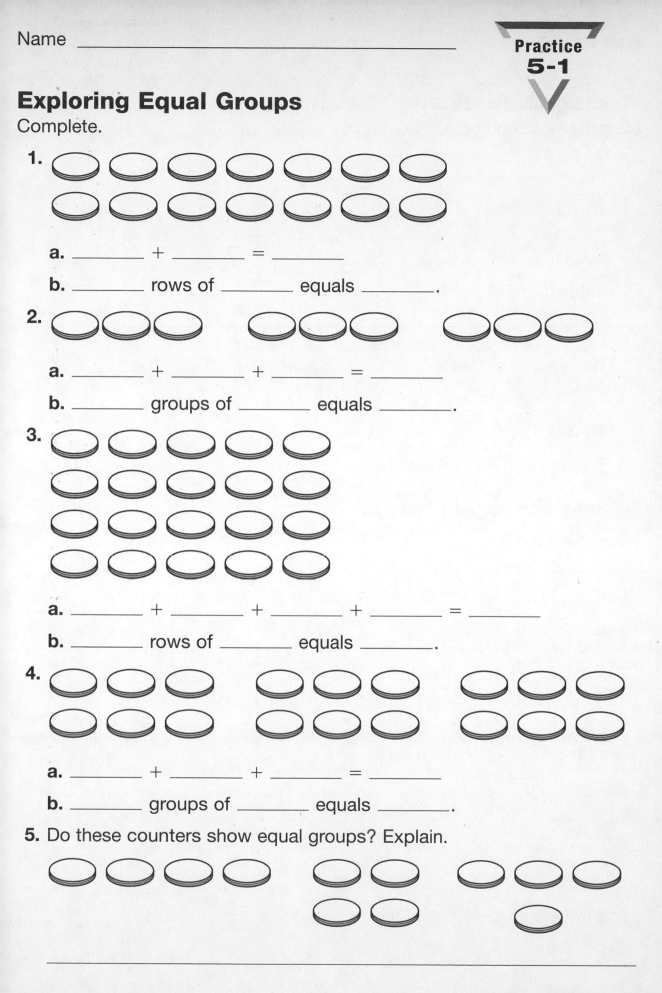

1.

   a. _____ + _____ = _____

   b. _____ rows of _____ equals _____.

2.

   a. _____ + _____ + _____ = _____

   b. _____ groups of _____ equals _____.

3.

   a. _____ + _____ + _____ + _____ = _____

   b. _____ rows of _____ equals _____.

4.

   a. _____ + _____ + _____ = _____

   b. _____ groups of _____ equals _____.

5. Do these counters show equal groups? Explain.

Writing Multiplication Sentences

Complete each number sentence.

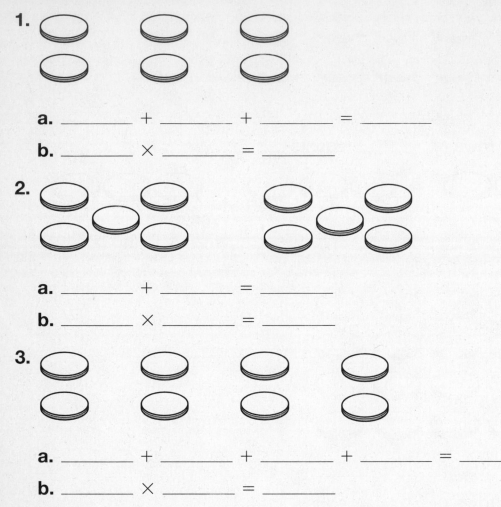

1.

    a. _____ + _____ + _____ = _____

    b. _____ × _____ = _____

2.

    a. _____ + _____ = _____

    b. _____ × _____ = _____

3.

    a. _____ + _____ + _____ + _____ = _____

    b. _____ × _____ = _____

4. Draw a picture that shows 3 × 4. Find the product.

5. Can you multiply to find the total of 9 + 9 + 9? Explain.

_____

6. Can you multiply to find the total of 3 + 4 + 5? Explain.

_____

Exploring Multiplication Stories

1. Is this a multiplication story? Explain.

Sam makes shirts. He sold 3 shirts one day, and 4 the next day. How many shirts did Sam sell?

_____

Write a multiplication story for **2–6**.
You may use counters to solve.

2. 2 × 5

_____

_____

3. 3 × 6

_____

_____

4. 4 × 4

_____

_____

5. 6 × 2

_____

_____

6. 6 × 4

_____

_____

Solve.

7. There are 6 cars in the parking lot. Each car has 4 tires. How many tires are there?

_____

Name _____

Review and Practice

Vocabulary Match each with its definition.

_____ 1. product   **a.** one of the numbers multiplied

_____ 2. factor   **b.** an arrangement of rows and columns

_____ 3. array   **c.** the number obtained by multiplying
                                   numbers

(Lessons 1 and 2) Complete.

4.

5.

a. ☐ + ☐ + ☐ + ☐ = ☐   **a.** ☐ + ☐ = ☐

b. ☐ groups of ☐ equals ☐.   **b.** ☐ groups of ☐ equals ☐.

c. ☐ × ☐ = ☐   **c.** ☐ × ☐ = ☐

6. Idaho has 2 representatives in the House of
   Representatives. Minnesota has 4 times as many.
   How many representatives does Minnesota have?

   _____

7. Is the product of 7 × 3 the same as the product of
   3 × 7? Explain.

   _____

   _____

(Lesson 3) Write a multiplication story for each.
You may use counters to solve.

8. $4 \times 5 =$ _____

   _____

9. $3 \times 7 =$ _____

   _____

(Mixed Review) Add or subtract.

10. $23 + 17 =$ _____   11. $45 - 20 =$ _____   12. $58 + 26 =$ _____

2 as a Factor

Find each product.

1. $3 \times 2 =$ _____   **2.** $5 \times 2 =$ _____

3. $2 \times 1 =$ _____   **4.** $2 \times 10 =$ _____

5. $2 \times 9 =$ _____   **6.** $8 \times 2 =$ _____

7. $4 \times 2 =$ _____   **8.** $6 \times 2 =$ _____

9. $2 \times 2 =$ _____   **10.** $2 \times 7 =$ _____

11.	**12.**	**13.**	**14.**	**15.**
4 $\times\,2$	2 $\times\,5$	6 $\times\,2$	8 $\times\,2$	9 $\times\,2$

16.	**17.**	**18.**	**19.**	**20.**
10 $\times\,\,2$	7 $\times\,2$	2 $\times\,1$	2 $\times\,3$	10 $\times\,\,2$

21. Find the product of 5 and 2. _____

22. Find the product of 2 and 8. _____

23. Find the product of 10 and 2. _____

24. Find the product of 6 and 2. _____

25. Find the product of 7 and 2. _____

26. Find the product of 3 and 2. _____

27. Is the product of 5 and 2 the same as the sum of 5
and 2? Explain.

_____

28. Draw a picture to show that 7×2 is the same as 2×7.

5 as a Factor

Find each product.

1. $2 \times 5 =$ _____   2. $5 \times 5 =$ _____

3. $5 \times 1 =$ _____   4. $5 \times 8 =$ _____

5. $2 \times 9 =$ _____   6. $3 \times 5 =$ _____

7. $5 \times 4 =$ _____   8. $5 \times 6 =$ _____

9. $5 \times 7 =$ _____   10. $2 \times 8 =$ _____

11.	12.	13.	14.	15.
4	5	6	5	9
$\times\ 5$	$\times\ 5$	$\times\ 2$	$\times\ 8$	$\times\ 5$

16.	17.	18.	19.	20.
8	7	2	2	8
$\times\ 2$	$\times\ 2$	$\times\ 1$	$\times\ 3$	$\times\ 5$

21.	22.	23.	24.	25.
5	7	8	6	3
$\times\ 2$	$\times\ 5$	$\times\ 5$	$\times\ 5$	$\times\ 5$

26. Find the product of 5 and 7. _____

27. Multiply 8 by 5. _____

28. If you know the product of 8 and 5, how can you use it to find 9×5?

_____

29. Is 7×5 greater or less than 8×5? Explain.

_____

Exploring Patterns on a
Hundred Chart: 2s and 5s

Finish these sentences.

1. a. Multiples of 2 always end in _____.

  b. Write some multiplication sentences to show the pattern:

  _____

2. a. Multiples of 5 always end in _____.

  b. Write some multiplication sentences to show the pattern:

  _____

Find each product.

3. $8 \times 2 =$ _____   **4.** $8 \times 5 =$ _____   **5.** $2 \times 2 =$ _____

6. $7 \times 5 =$ _____   **7.** $2 \times 7 =$ _____   **8.** $5 \times 4 =$ _____

9. $6 \times 5 =$ _____   **10.** $2 \times 9 =$ _____   **11.** $2 \times 10 =$ _____

12. $\begin{array}{r} 4 \\ \times\, 2 \\ \hline \end{array}$ **13.** $\begin{array}{r} 6 \\ \times\, 2 \\ \hline \end{array}$ **14.** $\begin{array}{r} 9 \\ \times\, 5 \\ \hline \end{array}$ **15.** $\begin{array}{r} 2 \\ \times\, 1 \\ \hline \end{array}$

16. $\begin{array}{r} 5 \\ \times\, 6 \\ \hline \end{array}$ **17.** $\begin{array}{r} 3 \\ \times\, 2 \\ \hline \end{array}$ **18.** $\begin{array}{r} 5 \\ \times\, 1 \\ \hline \end{array}$ **19.** $\begin{array}{r} 2 \\ \times\, 5 \\ \hline \end{array}$

20. Find the product of 5 and 3. _____

21. Multiply 6 by 2. _____

22. What numbers are shaded twice when you shade
multiples of 2s and multiples of 5s on a hundred chart?

_____

Exploring 0 and 1 as Factors

Finish these sentences.

1. a. The product of any number and 1 is _____.

   b. Write a multiplication sentence to show this.

   _____

2. a. The product of any number and 0 is _____.

   b. Write a multiplication sentence to show this.

   _____

Find each product.

3. $8 \times 0 =$ _____ 4. $8 \times 1 =$ _____ 5. $0 \times 2 =$ _____

6. $1 \times 5 =$ _____ 7. $2 \times 1 =$ _____ 8. $5 \times 4 =$ _____

9. $5 \times 5 =$ _____ 10. $2 \times 9 =$ _____

11. $\begin{array}{r} 4 \\ \times\, 2 \\ \hline \end{array}$ 12. $\begin{array}{r} 6 \\ \times\, 1 \\ \hline \end{array}$ 13. $\begin{array}{r} 9 \\ \times\, 0 \\ \hline \end{array}$ 14. $\begin{array}{r} 2 \\ \times\, 1 \\ \hline \end{array}$

15. $\begin{array}{r} 1 \\ \times\, 6 \\ \hline \end{array}$ 16. $\begin{array}{r} 3 \\ \times\, 2 \\ \hline \end{array}$ 17. $\begin{array}{r} 5 \\ \times\, 1 \\ \hline \end{array}$ 18. $\begin{array}{r} 1 \\ \times\, 5 \\ \hline \end{array}$

19. $\begin{array}{r} 0 \\ \times\, 3 \\ \hline \end{array}$ 20. $\begin{array}{r} 1 \\ \times\, 3 \\ \hline \end{array}$ 21. $\begin{array}{r} 0 \\ \times\, 1 \\ \hline \end{array}$ 22. $\begin{array}{r} 0 \\ \times\, 0 \\ \hline \end{array}$

23. Find the product of 1 and 1. _____

24. Multiply 0 by 1. _____

Complete. Write $\times$ or $+$.

25. 8 _____ $1 = 9$ 26. 9 _____ $1 = 9$ 27. 0 _____ $5 = 5$

28. 2 _____ $10 = 20$ 29. 2 _____ $0 = 0$ 30. 5 _____ $5 = 10$

9 as a Factor

Find each product.

1. $9 \times 8 =$ _____   **2.** $4 \times 9 =$ _____   **3.** $9 \times 7 =$ _____

4. $9 \times 6 =$ _____   **5.** $5 \times 9 =$ _____   **6.** $0 \times 5 =$ _____

7. $9 \times 3 =$ _____   **8.** $3 \times 5 =$ _____   **9.** $2 \times 6 =$ _____

10.   9
   $\times\ 9$

11.   8
   $\times\ 5$

12.   2
   $\times\ 7$

13.   9
   $\times\ 8$

14.   5
   $\times\ 4$

15.   1
   $\times\ 9$

16.   7
   $\times\ 5$

17.   9
   $\times\ 0$

18. Find the product of 8 and 9. _____

19. Multiply 9 by 2. _____

20. If you forget the product of 9 and 9, what can you do to figure it out?

_____

_____

21. Is 6×9 the same as 9×7? Explain.

_____

22. Is 5×9 the same as 6×9? Explain.

_____

23. Write a number sentence that shows the same product as the product of 9 and 2.

_____

Analyze Word Problems: Too Much or Too Little Information

Decide if the problem has too much or too little information.
Then solve. If there is not enough information, tell what
information is needed.

1. It takes about 3 months to grow tomatoes. The vines
   should be planted about 2 feet apart and get a lot of sun.
   If Taylor wants to plant 6 tomato vines in a row, how long
   should the row be?

   Too much or too little information? _____

   How do you solve it? _____

   _____

2. Each tomato vine can grow about 25 tomatoes. Taylor
   wants to make 3 gallons of spaghetti sauce with his
   tomatoes. Will 6 vines be enough?

   Too much or too little information? _____

   How do you solve it? _____

   _____

3. Kathryn is going to knit a sweater that is red and yellow.
   She needs 6 skeins of red yarn. If each skein is 100
   meters long, how many meters of yarn will she need
   all together?

   Too much or too little information? _____

   How do you solve it? _____

   _____

4. A piano keyboard has a total of 88 black and white
   keys. 36 of these are black. It takes 13 keys to play an
   octave. How many keys are white?

   Too much or too little information? _____

   How do you solve it? _____

   _____

Analyze Strategies: Draw a Picture

Draw a picture to help you solve.

1. How many bricks will Julia need to build
   a garden wall 9 bricks long and 8 bricks high? _____

2. Julia wants to build another garden wall,
   10 bricks long and 3 bricks high. Can she
   build it with red and white bricks, so that no
   two bricks of the same color are next to each other? _____

Draw a picture or use any strategy to solve the problems.

3. Ray is setting the table for a birthday dinner. He needs to
   set 12 places at a round table. He has 3 different kinds
   of plates: white plates; blue plates; and gold plates. How
   can he set the table so that no two of the same kind of
   plates are next to each other?

   _____

4. Ray has 13 forks, 15 spoons, and 11 dinner knives. If
   12 people are coming to dinner does he have enough
   silverware so that each person can have a fork, spoon
   and dinner knife?

   _____

Name _____

Review and Practice

(Lessons 4–8) Find each product.

1.	3	2.	5	3.	8	4.	4	5.	9
	× 2		× 8		× 2		× 9		× 0

6.	5	7.	9	8.	1	9.	5	10.	7
	× 7		× 2		× 5		× 2		× 2

11. $3 \times 5 =$ _____   **12.** $1 \times 2 =$ _____

13. $6 \times 2 =$ _____   **14.** $9 \times 5 =$ _____

15. $5 \times 4 =$ _____   **16.** $2 \times 2 =$ _____

17. List 5 multiples of 3. _____

(Lessons 9 and 10) Solve.

18. Harold gave each of his nine friends
three stickers. Four of the stickers were
red. How many stickers did he give away? _____

19. Pamela has 2 boxes of crayons. Each box
has 48 crayons in it. 8 of the crayons are
sharpened. How many crayons does she have? _____

20. Michele and 2 friends each live on a
different floor of a three-story apartment
building. Shaun lives above Barb and
below Michele. Who lives on the first floor? _____

(Mixed Review) Continue each pattern.

21. 7, 14, 21, 28, _____, _____, _____

22. 18, 27, 36, 45, _____, _____, _____

23. 10, 12, 14, 16, _____, _____, _____

Name _____

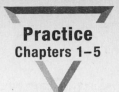
Cumulative Review
(Chapter 3, Lesson 13) Solve.

1. Sue Ann has $3.50 in quarters and $1.15 in nickels. How many quarters does she have? How many nickels? How much money does she have in all?

_____

(Chapter 2, Lesson 7) Write each set of numbers in order from greatest to least.

2. 470, 704, 740, 407 _____

3. 400,100; 410,000; 401,700; 407,100

_____

(Chapter 3, Lesson 7) Find each sum.

4. 326	**5.** 412	**6.** 319	**7.** 828
+ 719	+ 811	+ 324	+ 124

(Chapter 4, Lesson 10) Find each difference.

8. 314	**9.** 427	**10.** 516	**11.** 644
– 126	– 189	– 427	– 356

12. 818 – 529 = _____   **13.** 745 – 266 = _____

(Chapter 5, Lessons 4 and 5) Find each product.

14. 3	**15.** 4	**16.** 5	**17.** 2	**18.** 6
× 5	× 2	× 8	× 9	× 5

19. 7 × 5 = _____   **20.** 2 × 6 = _____   **21.** 7 × 2 = _____

Name _____

3 as a Factor: Using Known Facts

Find each product.

1. 8
   $\times 3$

2. 3
   $\times 1$

3. 6
   $\times 3$

4. 7
   $\times 3$

5. 3
   $\times 2$

6. 3
   $\times 3$

7. 4
   $\times 3$

8. 9
   $\times 3$

9. 3
   $\times 8$

10. 5
   $\times 3$

11. 3×2 _____

12. 6×3 _____

13. 3×5 _____

14. 3×9 _____

15. 8×3 _____

16. 1×3 _____

17. 7×3 _____

18. 4×3 _____

19. What is the product of 9 and 3? _____

20. What is the product of 6 and 3? _____

21. Multiply 5 by 3. _____

22. Multiply 3 by 4. _____

23. If you know the product of 2×6, how can you find the product of 3×6? What is it?

_____

24. Tim says, "To find 3×8, I can find 2×8 and add one more group of 3." What's wrong? Explain.

_____

4 as a Factor: Doubling

Find each product.

1. $\begin{array}{r} 4 \\ \times\ 5 \\ \hline \end{array}$
2. $\begin{array}{r} 6 \\ \times\ 4 \\ \hline \end{array}$
3. $\begin{array}{r} 9 \\ \times\ 4 \\ \hline \end{array}$
4. $\begin{array}{r} 4 \\ \times\ 3 \\ \hline \end{array}$
5. $\begin{array}{r} 1 \\ \times\ 4 \\ \hline \end{array}$

6. $\begin{array}{r} 8 \\ \times\ 2 \\ \hline \end{array}$
7. $\begin{array}{r} 4 \\ \times\ 8 \\ \hline \end{array}$
8. $\begin{array}{r} 4 \\ \times\ 4 \\ \hline \end{array}$
9. $\begin{array}{r} 2 \\ \times\ 4 \\ \hline \end{array}$
10. $\begin{array}{r} 4 \\ \times\ 7 \\ \hline \end{array}$

11. 5×4 _____

12. 4×9 _____

13. 4×2 _____

14. 4×4 _____

15. 1×4 _____

16. 6×4 _____

17. 3×4 _____

18. 7×4 _____

19. Multiply 8 by 4. _____

20. Multiply 4 by 7. _____

21. What is the product of 4 and 9? _____

22. What is the product of 4 and 5? _____

23. Draw arrays to show that 4×5 is the same as 5×4.

24. Could you use doubling to multiply 7×3? Explain.

_____

_____

6 as a Factor: Using Known Facts

Find each product.

1. 0 × 6	2. 3 × 6	3. 6 × 5	4. 9 × 6	5. 6 × 6

6. 6 × 2	7. 1 × 6	8. 7 × 6	9. 6 × 4	10. 6 × 8

11. 6×4　　　　**12.** 2×6　　　　**13.** 9×6　　　　**14.** 6×0

_____　　　　_____　　　　_____　　　　_____

15. 5×6　　　　**16.** 6×8　　　　**17.** 6×6　　　　**18.** 3×6

_____　　　　_____　　　　_____　　　　_____

19. Find the product of 6 and 7.　　　**20.** What is 9 multiplied by 6?

_____　　　　　　　　　　　　_____

21. Find the product of 6 and 6.　　　**22.** What is 3 multiplied by 6?

_____　　　　　　　　　　　　_____

23. Which is greater, 6×9 or 9×5? How can you tell without multiplying?

24. Can you think of a way to use doubling to multiply 6×7? Explain.

_____　　　_____

_____　　　_____

7 and 8 as Factors

Find each product.

1. $\begin{array}{r} 7 \\ \times\ 8 \\ \hline \end{array}$
2. $\begin{array}{r} 8 \\ \times\ 9 \\ \hline \end{array}$
3. $\begin{array}{r} 9 \\ \times\ 7 \\ \hline \end{array}$
4. $\begin{array}{r} 6 \\ \times\ 8 \\ \hline \end{array}$
5. $\begin{array}{r} 4 \\ \times\ 8 \\ \hline \end{array}$

6. $\begin{array}{r} 3 \\ \times\ 7 \\ \hline \end{array}$
7. $\begin{array}{r} 7 \\ \times\ 7 \\ \hline \end{array}$
8. $\begin{array}{r} 5 \\ \times\ 8 \\ \hline \end{array}$
9. $\begin{array}{r} 8 \\ \times\ 8 \\ \hline \end{array}$
10. $\begin{array}{r} 4 \\ \times\ 7 \\ \hline \end{array}$

11. 6×7 _____

12. 8×7 _____

13. 0×7 _____

14. 8×2 _____

15. 8×0 _____

16. 7×7 _____

17. 2×7 _____

18. 9×7 _____

19. Find the product of 8 and 9.

_____

20. Find the product of 7 and 6.

_____

21. Find the product of 7 and 8.

_____

22. Find the product of 8 and 5.

_____

23. How could you find the product of 7×8 if you know the product of 5×8?

_____

_____

24. How can you tell that 7×6 is greater than 6×5 without multiplying?

_____

_____

Decision Making

Annie is a party planner. She must plan the menu for 3 dinners; one for 4 people, one for 7 people, and one for 8 people. She needs to make a table to find out how many of each item will be needed for each dinner.

Complete the table.

Number per Serving	4-Person Dinner	7-Person Dinner	8-Person Dinner
6 snack crackers	24	42	48
4 potatoes			
2 chicken pieces			
7 baby carrots			
3 broccoli spears			
8 parsley sprigs			
7 strawberries			
1 mint			

1. How many baby carrots will Annie need for the 8-person dinner? _____

2. How many chicken pieces will she need for the 7-person dinner? _____

3. Annie decides she wants to serve cream with the strawberries. She needs 3 spoonfuls for each person. How many spoonfuls does she need for:

   a. the 4-person dinner? _____

   b. the 7-person dinner? _____

   c. the 8-person dinner? _____

4. One of the people at the 7-person dinner can't go. How many chicken pieces will Annie need for that dinner now? _____

5. An extra person will be going to the 4-person dinner. How many strawberries will Annie need for that dinner now? _____

Review and Practice

(Lesson 1) Find each product.

1. $5 \times 3 =$ _____

2. $3 \times 2 =$ _____

3. $6 \times 3 =$ _____

4. $7 \times 3 =$ _____

5. Leo wants to make 3 apple pies. The recipe calls for

4 apples per pie. How many apples will he need? _____

(Lesson 2) Find each product.

6. $5 \times 4 =$ _____

7. $6 \times 4 =$ _____

8. $4 \times 4 =$ _____

9. $4 \times 9 =$ _____

10. Joel bought 4 boxes of note pads. Each box contained

8 note pads. How many notepads did Joel buy? _____

(Lesson 3) Find each product.

11. $9 \times 6 =$ _____

12. $3 \times 6 =$ _____

13. $6 \times 8 =$ _____

14. $6 \times 0 =$ _____

15. Each actor receives 6 free passes to each show. There

are 7 shows. How many free passes does each actor

receive? _____

(Lesson 4) Find each product.

16. $7 \times 6 =$ _____

17. $8 \times 3 =$ _____

18. $9 \times 8 =$ _____

19. $8 \times 7 =$ _____

20. $7 \times 7 =$ _____

21. $8 \times 8 =$ _____

(Mixed Review) Find each sum or difference.

22.
$$612$$
$$+839$$

23.
$$948$$
$$-479$$

24.
$$177$$
$$-91$$

25.
$$608$$
$$+55$$

Exploring Patterns on a Hundred Chart: 3s and 6s

1	2	3	4	5	6	7	8	9	10
11	12	13	14	15	16	17	18	19	20
21	22	23	24	25	26	27	28	29	30
31	32	33	34	35	36	37	38	39	40
41	42	43	44	45	46	47	48	49	50
51	52	53	54	55	56	57	58	59	60

1	2	3	4	5	6	7	8	9	10
11	12	13	14	15	16	17	18	19	20
21	22	23	24	25	26	27	28	29	30
31	32	33	34	35	36	37	38	39	40
41	42	43	44	45	46	47	48	49	50
51	52	53	54	55	56	57	58	59	60

1. What is the sum of the digits in each multiple of 3?

_____

2. How can you tell if a number is a multiple of 6?

_____

_____

Find each missing number. You may use a hundred chart to help.

3. $3 \times \square = 18$ **4.** $\square \times 3 = 9$

5. $6 \times \square = 36$ **6.** $\square \times 9 = 54$

7. $\square \times 8 = 48$ **8.** $3 \times \square = 18$

Write true or false. If the answer is false, explain why.

9. 34 is a multiple of 3.

_____

10. 24 is a multiple of 3 and 6.

_____

11. 16 is not a multiple of 6 or 3.

_____

Name _____

Exploring Patterns on a Fact Table

Look for patterns in multiples of greater numbers.

1. What is the pattern for multiples of 10?

_____

2. What is the pattern for multiples of 11?

_____

3. What is the pattern for multiples of 12?

_____

Find each product.

4. 9×9 **5.** 7×8 **6.** 6×12

_____   _____   _____

7. 10×11 **8.** 8×5 **9.** 7×9

_____   _____   _____

10. 12×7 **11.** 11×11 **12.** 12×6

_____   _____   _____

13. 7×10 **14.** 12×9 **15.** 11×3

_____   _____   _____

Continue each pattern.

16. 33, 44, 55, _____, _____, _____

17. 72, 60, 48, _____, _____, _____

18. 0, 20, 40, _____, _____, _____

19. 132, 110, 88, _____, _____, _____

20. 48, 60, 72, _____, _____, _____

Multiplying with 3 Factors

Find each product.

1. $(4 \times 3) \times 2$ **2.** $1 \times (6 \times 8)$ **3.** $9 \times 1 \times 7$

_____   _____   _____

4. $5 \times (3 \times 3)$ **5.** $2 \times 1 \times 5$ **6.** $(0 \times 1) \times 8$

_____   _____   _____

7. $2 \times 0 \times 9$ **8.** $3 \times (2 \times 5)$ **9.** $6 \times (6 \times 1)$

_____   _____   _____

10. $(3 \times 2) \times 7$ **11.** $1 \times 7 \times 4$ **12.** $(2 \times 0) \times 8$

_____   _____   _____

13. $(3 \times 6) \times 0$ **14.** $(2 \times 12) \times 1$ **15.** $6 \times 3 \times 3$

_____   _____   _____

16. Find the product of 1, 7, and 6. _____

17. Find the product of 9, 4, and 0. _____

18. Does 6×4 have the same product as $3 \times 4 \times 2$? Explain.

_____

_____

19. If you know the product of $5 \times 2 \times 3$, do you also know
the product of $3 \times 2 \times 5$? Explain.

_____

_____

Name _____

Compare Strategies: Look for a Pattern and Draw a Picture

Use any strategy to solve each problem.

1. Suppose you are planning a picnic for 34 people. You must buy paper plates in packages of 8. How many packages of paper plates will you need? _____

2. One package of rolls has enough rolls for 8 burgers. How many packages of rolls do you need for 25 burgers? _____

3. Your softball team has a party. Everyone uses 4 napkins. If there are 13 people at the party, how many napkins were used? _____

4. One loaf of bread makes 10 sandwiches. How many loaves do you need to make 54 sandwiches?

   _____

5. You are making pizza for a party. Each pizza has 8 slices.
   a. If 93 people will be at the party, how many pizzas should you make so that each person gets one slice?

   _____

   b. How many slices will be left over? _____

6. Each jug of juice serves 12 people. How many jugs will you need for 60 people? _____

Review and Practice

(Lesson 6) Write true or false. You may use a hundred chart to help.

1. 42 is a multiple of 6. _____

2. 41 is a multiple of 3. _____

3. 83 is a multiple of 3 and 6. _____

4. All multiples of 6 are also multiples of 3. _____

(Lesson 7) Continue each pattern.

5. 18, 27, 36, _____, _____, _____

6. 36, 48, 60, _____, _____, _____

7. How can you tell without multiplying that 6×10 does not equal 66?

_____

(Lesson 8) Find each product.

8. $5 \times 2 \times 8 =$ _____

9. $1 \times 9 \times 4 =$ _____

10. $0 \times 7 \times 1 =$ _____

11. $3 \times 2 \times 7 =$ _____

12. $2 \times (2 \times 3) =$ _____

13. $(6 \times 1) \times 5 =$ _____

(Lesson 9) Solve. Use any strategy.

14. You want to send cards to 37 people. The cards you want to send come in packages of 6. How many packages will you need? _____

15. While on vacation Marsha sent 35 postcards. She sent 7 postcards from each city she visited. How many cities did she visit? _____

(Mixed Review) Continue each pattern.

16. 48, 45, 42, _____, _____, _____

17. 6, 10, 14, 18, _____, _____, _____

18. 12, 24, 36, _____, _____, _____

Cumulative Review

(Chapter 3 Lesson 9) Find each sum.

1. $\begin{array}{r} 35 \\ 66 \\ +88 \\ \hline \end{array}$
2. $\begin{array}{r} 84 \\ 28 \\ +53 \\ \hline \end{array}$
3. $\begin{array}{r} 679 \\ 44 \\ +345 \\ \hline \end{array}$
4. $\begin{array}{r} 71 \\ 93 \\ +309 \\ \hline \end{array}$

5. Patricia earned 96, 95, and 87 on three math tests. She needs a total of 279 points to get an A average. Does she have enough points for an A? Explain.

_____

(Chapter 4 Lesson 11) Find each difference.

6. $\begin{array}{r} 800 \\ -\ \ 58 \\ \hline \end{array}$
7. $\begin{array}{r} 907 \\ -628 \\ \hline \end{array}$
8. $\begin{array}{r} 600 \\ -299 \\ \hline \end{array}$
9. $\begin{array}{r} 200 \\ -184 \\ \hline \end{array}$

(Chapter 5 Lesson 4) Find each product.

10. $\begin{array}{r} 8 \\ \times 2 \\ \hline \end{array}$
11. $\begin{array}{r} 2 \\ \times 4 \\ \hline \end{array}$
12. $\begin{array}{r} 2 \\ \times 5 \\ \hline \end{array}$
13. $\begin{array}{r} 7 \\ \times 2 \\ \hline \end{array}$
14. $\begin{array}{r} 9 \\ \times 2 \\ \hline \end{array}$

(Chapter 6 Lessons 1–3) Find each product.

15. $\begin{array}{r} 3 \\ \times 2 \\ \hline \end{array}$
16. $\begin{array}{r} 4 \\ \times 3 \\ \hline \end{array}$
17. $\begin{array}{r} 4 \\ \times 5 \\ \hline \end{array}$
18. $\begin{array}{r} 7 \\ \times 4 \\ \hline \end{array}$
19. $\begin{array}{r} 9 \\ \times 6 \\ \hline \end{array}$

20. $\begin{array}{r} 8 \\ \times 3 \\ \hline \end{array}$
21. $\begin{array}{r} 6 \\ \times 4 \\ \hline \end{array}$
22. $\begin{array}{r} 3 \\ \times 6 \\ \hline \end{array}$
23. $\begin{array}{r} 7 \\ \times 6 \\ \hline \end{array}$
24. $\begin{array}{r} 9 \\ \times 3 \\ \hline \end{array}$

Exploring Division as Sharing

Mrs. Robbins and Mrs. Siani are making up flower baskets for a wedding celebration. They have to do 6 baskets in all. They decide to share the work equally. How many baskets will each prepare?

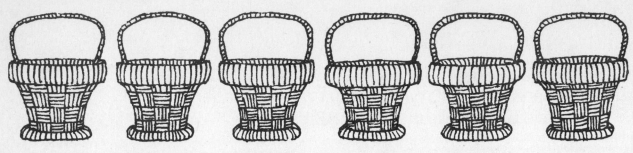

1. Draw a line to divide the baskets into 2 equal groups.

2. 6 flower baskets ÷ 2 women = _____ baskets each.

Complete. You may use counters or draw pictures to help.

3. 8 ÷ 2 = _____

4. 16 ÷ 4 = _____

Solve. You may use counters or draw pictures to help.

5. Misha and Angie have volunteered to call 10 people to raise money for their Girl Scout troop. If they divide the calls equally, how many calls will each girl make?

_____

6. You are helping the school yearbook editor. There are 24 pictures that will go on 3 pages in the yearbook. How many photos will you put on each page if you divide them evenly?

_____

Exploring Division as Repeated Subtraction

Maria is pouring glasses of iced tea. She has 18 ice cubes. If she wants to put 6 ice cubes in each glass, how many glasses can she fill?

1. Draw lines to show 6 ice cubes per glass.

2. 18 ice cubes ÷ 6 per glass = _____ glasses.

Complete. You may use counters or complete the pictures to help.

3. 10 letters

2 in each mailbox

10 ÷ 2 = _____

4. 12 flowers

3 in each pot

12 ÷ 3 = _____

5. Brenda puts 3 cookies on each plate. Can she make 5 plates with 15 cookies? Draw a picture and explain.

Exploring Division Stories

1. Three friends share a 6-pack of juice equally. How many cans of juice does each one drink?

$6 \div 3 =$ _____ cans

2. Telia made 15 snowflake ornaments. If she gives 3 to each of her friends, how many friends will get ornaments?

$15 \div 3 =$ _____ friends

Write a division story for each. You may use counters to solve.

3. $8 \div 4 =$ _____

_____

_____

4. $21 \div 7 =$ _____

_____

_____

Complete each number sentence. You may use counters to solve.

5. $16 \div$ _____ $= 2$ **6.** $24 \div$ _____ $= 8$ **7.** $36 \div$ _____ $= 4$

Solve. You may use counters or draw pictures to help.

8. Dana has 10 free show tickets. He can give away 2 to each person in his family. How many people are in his family?

_____

9. Beth's book has 28 pages. She reads 4 pages each day. How long will it take her to finish the book?   _____

10. Michael used 12 slices of cheese to make 4 equal-sized sandwiches. How many slices of cheese did he put in each sandwich?   _____

Name _____

Review and Practice

(Lessons 1 and 2) Use the pictures to help you complete each number sentence.

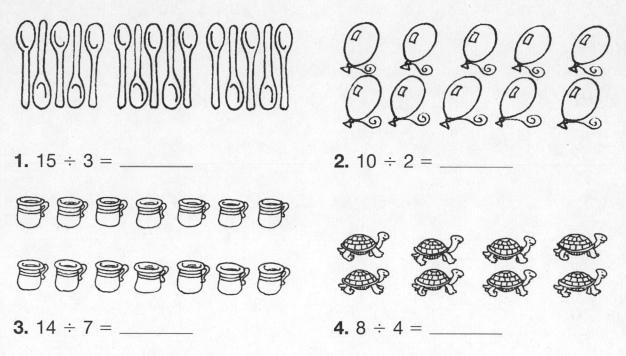

1. 15 ÷ 3 = _____

2. 10 ÷ 2 = _____

3. 14 ÷ 7 = _____

4. 8 ÷ 4 = _____

5. Natalie and her two brothers have $12 to spend on lunch. One Kid's Meal costs $3. Do they have enough money? Explain how you know.

_____

(Lesson 3) Write a division story for each. You may use counters to solve.

6. 20 ÷ 4 = _____

_____

_____

7. 18 ÷ 9 = _____

_____

_____

(Mixed Review) Complete each number sentence.

8. _____ + 8 = 13   **9.** _____ − 9 = 5   **10.** 6 + _____ = 11

Connecting Multiplication and Division

Complete. You may use counters to help.

1. $7 \times$ _____ $= 28$

$28 \div 7 =$ _____

2. $6 \times$ _____ $= 42$

$42 \div 6 =$ _____

3. $2 \times$ _____ $= 12$

$12 \div 2 =$ _____

4. $2 \times$ _____ $= 18$

$18 \div 2 =$ _____

5. $3 \times$ _____ $= 21$

$21 \div 3 =$ _____

6. $7 \times$ _____ $= 35$

$35 \div 7 =$ _____

7. $2 \times$ _____ $= 6$

$6 \div 2 =$ _____

8. $5 \times$ _____ $= 25$

$25 \div 5 =$ _____

9. $6 \times$ _____ $= 12$

$12 \div 6 =$ _____

10. $4 \times$ _____ $= 32$

$32 \div 4 =$ _____

11. $3 \times$ _____ $= 30$

$30 \div 3 =$ _____

12. $8 \times$ _____ $= 24$

$24 \div 8 =$ _____

13. What multiplication fact could you use to solve $24 \div 3$?

_____

14. What are the number sentences in the fact family
with $32 \div 4 = 8$?

_____

15. What multiplication fact could you use to solve $20 \div 2$?

_____

16. What are the number sentences in the fact family
with $24 \div 4 = 6$?

_____

Name _____

Dividing by 2
Find each quotient.

1. $2\overline{)10}$ **2.** $2\overline{)4}$ **3.** $2\overline{)16}$ **4.** $2\overline{)18}$

5. $6 \div 2 =$ _____ **6.** $2 \div 2 =$ _____
7. $8 \div 2 =$ _____ **8.** $4 \div 2 =$ _____

9. Divide 12 by 2. _____ **10.** Divide 14 by 2. _____

11. How can you use multiplication to help you find $18 \div 2$?

_____

12. Nancy says, "I can solve $6 \div 2$ using the fact
$6 \times 2 = 12$." Do you agree or disagee? Explain.

_____

13. Ben says, "I can solve $16 \div 2$ by using the fact
$2 \times 8 = 16$." Do you agree or disagree? Explain.

_____

14. How can you use multiplication to help you find $8 \div 2$?

_____

15. How can you use multiplication to help you find $14 \div 7$?

_____

16. Use multiplication facts to help you find:

    a. $20 \div 2$ _____

    b. $16 \div 2$ _____

    c. $12 \div 2$ _____

Dividing by 5

Find each quotient.

1. $5\overline{)15}$ **2.** $5\overline{)25}$

3. $5\overline{)10}$ **4.** $5\overline{)30}$

5. $2\overline{)8}$ **6.** $5\overline{)40}$

7. $5\overline{)35}$ **8.** $2\overline{)12}$

9. $45 \div 5 =$ _____   **10.** $20 \div 5 =$ _____

11. $25 \div 5 =$ _____   **12.** $30 \div 5 =$ _____

13. $16 \div 2 =$ _____   **14.** $10 \div 5 =$ _____

15. $15 \div 5 =$ _____   **16.** $45 \div 5 =$ _____

17. Divide 20 by 5. _____

18. What multiplication fact can help you find $5\overline{)40}$?

_____

19. What multiplication fact can help you find $2\overline{)14}$?

_____

20. What multiplication fact can help you find $45 \div 5$?

_____

21. What multiplication fact can help you find $10 \div 2$?

_____

22. How could you take away groups of 5 to find $25 \div 5$?

_____

_____

Dividing by 3 and 4

Find each quotient.

1. $3\overline{)15}$ **2.** $4\overline{)8}$ **3.** $4\overline{)12}$

4. $5\overline{)30}$ **5.** $3\overline{)6}$ **6.** $3\overline{)21}$

7. $4\overline{)28}$ **8.** $4\overline{)20}$ **9.** $3\overline{)12}$

10. $2\overline{)10}$ **11.** $3\overline{)18}$ **12.** $4\overline{)32}$

13. $27 \div 3 =$ _____   **14.** $9 \div 3 =$ _____

15. $24 \div 4 =$ _____   **16.** $24 \div 3 =$ _____

17. $25 \div 5 =$ _____   **18.** $16 \div 4 =$ _____

19. $14 \div 2 =$ _____   **20.** $36 \div 4 =$ _____

21. Divide 18 by 3. _____

22. Divide 20 by 4. _____

23. How many 4s are in 28? _____

24. How many 3s are in 15? _____

25. How many 4s are in 40? _____

26. How many 3s are in 30? _____

27. How could you take away equal groups to find $4\overline{)12}$?

_____

Exploring Dividing with 0 and 1

Find each quotient. Complete the division rule.

1. a. $3 \div 1 =$ _____

   b. Rule: Any number divided by 1 equals _____.

2. a. $5 \div 5 =$ _____

   b. Rule: Any number (except 0) divided by itself equals _____.

3. a. $0 \div 2 =$ _____

   b. Rule: Zero divided by any number (except 0) equals _____.

4. Can you divide by 0? _____

Find each quotient. Write the division rule that explains the answer.

5. $4 \div 4 =$ _____

   Rule: _____

6. $0 \div 7 =$ _____

   Rule: _____

7. $8 \div 1 =$ _____

   Rule: _____

Write >, <, or =.

8. $6 \div 6 \bigcirc 3 \div 3$ **9.** $12 \div 4 \bigcirc 12 \div 3$

10. $25 \div 5 \bigcirc 0 \div 5$ **11.** $4 \div 1 \bigcirc 6 \div 1$

12. $6 \div 2 \bigcirc 3 \div 1$ **13.** $0 \div 4 \bigcirc 4 \div 2$

14. $8 \div 4 \bigcirc 4 \div 2$ **15.** $10 \div 5 \bigcirc 5 \div 5$

Analyze Word Problems:
Choose an Operation

Which number sentence would you use to solve the problem? Explain.

1. Suppose Blair worked 6 hours a week for 3 weeks. How many hours did she work?

   A. $6 + 3 = 9$ **B.** $6 \times 3 = 18$ **C.** $6 - 3 = 3$ **D.** $18 + 6 = 24$

   _____

2. Marcie sold $8 worth of fruit tarts at a bake sale. Each tart cost $2. How many tarts did she sell?

   A. $8 - 2 = 6$ **B.** $8 \div 2 = 4$ **C.** $8 \times 2 = 16$ **D.** $8 + 2 = 10$

   _____

3. Arthur had 6 tickets to a concert. He gave 2 of them to Joe. How many tickets did he have left?

   A. $6 - 2 = 4$ **B.** $6 + 2 = 8$ **C.** $6 \times 2 = 12$ **D.** $6 \div 2 = 3$

   _____

Write which operation you would use. Then solve.

4. Zachary bought 4 bananas and 3 oranges. How many pieces of fruit did he buy?

   _____

5. Lars bought a 2-pound bag of dog food for $2.25 and a 1-pound bag of cat food for $1.54. How much money did he spend?

   _____

6. Isabella earns $4 per hour working at the pet store. If she works for 7 hours, how much money will she earn?

   _____

7. Nick had 16 marbles. He gave an equal number to each of 4 friends. How many marbles did each friend get?

   _____

Review and Practice

Vocabulary Write true or false for each statement.

1. In the problem $18 \div 2 = 9$, the divisor is 9. _____

2. Fact families are groups of related facts using the same set of digits. _____

3. The dividend in the problem $24 \div 3 = 8$ is 24. _____

4. The quotient in the problem $12 \div 4 = 3$ is 12. _____

(Lessons 5–8) Find each quotient.

5. $2 \div 2 =$ _____

6. $16 \div 4 =$ _____

7. $20 \div 5 =$ _____

8. $8 \div 2 =$ _____

9. $12 \div 3 =$ _____

10. $40 \div 5 =$ _____

11. $20 \div 4 =$ _____

12. $18 \div 3 =$ _____

13. $14 \div 2 =$ _____

14. $45 \div 5 =$ _____

15. $54 \div 1 =$ _____

16. $0 \div 2 =$ _____

17. $27 \div 3 =$ _____

18. $36 \div 4 =$ _____

19. $0 \div 4 =$ _____

20. $16 \div 2 =$ _____

21. $2\overline{)18}$

22. $5\overline{)30}$

23. $3\overline{)21}$

24. $4\overline{)8}$

(Lesson 9) Write which operation you would use. Then solve.

25. Selma wants to build bird houses to give as gifts. It takes 4 boards to make one house. Selma has 24 boards. How many bird houses can she make?

_____

26. Nu has to write 3 reports. Each report must be 2 pages. How many pages must he write?

_____

(Mixed Review) Find each missing factor.

27. $1 \times$ _____ $\times 8 = 0$

28. $3 \times$ _____ $\times 2 = 24$

29. _____ $\times 5 \times 2 = 20$

30. $4 \times 1 \times$ _____ $= 20$

Dividing by 6 and 7

Find each quotient.

1. $6\overline{)18}$ **2.** $7\overline{)14}$ **3.** $6\overline{)24}$

4. $7\overline{)28}$ **5.** $6\overline{)6}$ **6.** $1\overline{)7}$

7. $6\overline{)54}$ **8.** $7\overline{)49}$ **9.** $7\overline{)42}$

10. $3\overline{)18}$ **11.** $6\overline{)12}$ **12.** $6\overline{)36}$

13. $42 \div 6 =$ _____   **14.** $7 \div 7 =$ _____   **15.** $56 \div 7 =$ _____

16. $12 \div 6 =$ _____   **17.** $63 \div 7 =$ _____   **18.** $21 \div 3 =$ _____

19. $0 \div 6 =$ _____   **20.** $30 \div 5 =$ _____   **21.** $35 \div 7 =$ _____

22. $48 \div 6 =$ _____   **23.** $24 \div 4 =$ _____   **24.** $21 \div 7 =$ _____

25. Divide 36 by 6. _____   **26.** Divide 30 by 6. _____

27. Divide 28 by 4. _____   **28.** Divide 0 by 7. _____

29. What multiplication fact can help you find $42 \div 7$?

_____

30. What multiplication fact can help you find $24 \div 6$?

_____

31. Is the quotient of $48 \div 6$ greater than or less than the quotient of $42 \div 7$? Explain.

_____

32. Is the quotient of $63 \div 7$ greater than or less than the quotient of $54 \div 6$? Explain.

_____

Dividing by 8 and 9
Find each quotient.

1. $8\overline{)16}$ **2.** $9\overline{)36}$ **3.** $8\overline{)40}$

4. $9\overline{)36}$ **5.** $7\overline{)21}$ **6.** $8\overline{)8}$

7. $9\overline{)45}$ **8.** $8\overline{)72}$ **9.** $9\overline{)0}$

10. $4\overline{)36}$ **11.** $9\overline{)63}$ **12.** $8\overline{)56}$

13. $81 \div 9 =$ _____ **14.** $32 \div 8 =$ _____

15. $27 \div 9 =$ _____ **16.** $9 \div 9 =$ _____

17. $64 \div 8 =$ _____ **18.** $54 \div 9 =$ _____

19. $72 \div 9 =$ _____ **20.** $24 \div 8 =$ _____

21. Divide 56 by 8. _____ **22.** Divide 18 by 9. _____

23. Divide 45 by 9. _____ **24.** Divide 56 by 7. _____

25. What multiplication fact can help you find $63 \div 9$?

_____

26. What multiplication fact can help you find $48 \div 8$?

_____

27. How does knowing $4 \times 9 = 36$ help you solve $36 \div 9$?

_____

28. Which is greater, $48 \div 6$ or $48 \div 8$? Explain.

_____

29. Which is greater, $81 \div 9$ or $36 \div 4$?

_____

Exploring Even and Odd Numbers

1. Even numbers have 0, _____, 4, _____, or _____ in the ones place.

2. Odd numbers have 1, _____, _____, 7, or _____ in the ones place.

Write odd or even for each. You may use color cubes to help.

3. ☐☐☐ ☐☐☐☐
☐☐☐☐☐☐☐

_____

4. ☐☐☐☐☐☐
☐☐☐☐☐

_____

5. 6 _____

6. 19 _____

7. 9 _____

8. 24 _____

9. 18 _____

10. 17 _____

11. 11 _____

12. 23 _____

13. Start with 14 and name the next 5 even numbers. Explain how you know which numbers are even.

_____

_____

14. Add the pairs of odd numbers.
Do you get even or odd sums? _____

a. 7 + 5 _____   b. 3 + 9 _____   c. 11 + 7 _____

d. Can you think of any two odd numbers
where the sum of the numbers will be odd? _____

15. Add the pairs of even and odd numbers.
Do you get even or odd sums?   _____

a. 5 + 16 _____   b. 8 + 7 _____   c. 14 + 5 _____

d. Can you think of any two numbers, one even and
the other odd, in which the sum is an even number? _____

16. Tenisha has two pages in her photo album to fill. She puts 7 photos on each page. Did she have an even or odd number of photos?

Explain. _____

Compare Strategies: Use Objects and Make an Organized List

Use any strategy to solve.

1. Anita received 12 new stickers and a new sticker album on her birthday. She wants to put an equal number of stickers on each page that she uses.

   a. How many pages could Anita use in her sticker album?

   _____

   b. How many stickers could be on each page?

   _____

   c. List all the ways Anita could put the stickers in her sticker album.

   _____

   _____

2. Paul has a collection of action figures. He wants to arrange the figures in equal rows. If Paul has 30 action figures, what are all the ways to arrange the figures?

   _____

   _____

3. Juan has 2 pairs of sneakers, one black pair and one white pair. He has 3 baseball caps, one red, one blue and the other orange. What are all the combinations of shoes and caps he could wear?

   _____

   _____

   _____

4. Rosalind must read an 18-page book. She wants to read an equal number of pages every day. List all the possible ways she could divide her reading.

   _____

   _____

Exploring Algebra: Balancing Scales

Find all the ways to balance each scale. Make a table to record each way. You may use color cubes to help.

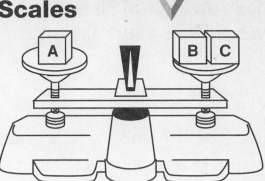

1. a. Box A has 8 cubes inside. How many cubes can be in boxes B and C?

Fill in the missing numbers in the table.

A	8	8	8	8	8	8	8	8	8
B	8	7							0
C	0		2	3					

b. 2 cubes have been removed from box A. How many cubes are now in the boxes? Fill in the missing numbers in the table.

A							
B		5			2		0
C	0			3			

2. Box B has 7 cubes inside. Box C has 5 cubes inside. How many cubes are in each box A?

_____

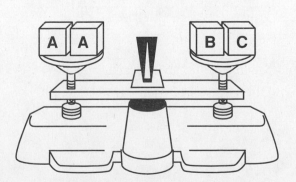

3. Box A has 15 cubes inside. How many cubes are in each box B?

_____

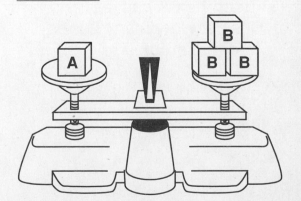

Name _____

Review and Practice

Vocabulary Match the set of numbers with the word describing it.

1. even _____   **a.** 26, 32, 24, 48

2. odd _____   **b.** 31, 47, 19, 21

(Lessons 10 and 11) Find each quotient.

3. 12 ÷ 6 = _____   4. 16 ÷ 8 = _____

5. 21 ÷ 7 = _____   6. 28 ÷ 7 = _____

7. 18 ÷ 9 = _____   8. 45 ÷ 9 = _____

9. 24 ÷ 8 = _____   10. 18 ÷ 6 = _____

11. Divide 49 by 7. _____   12. Divide 56 by 8. _____

(Lesson 12) Write odd or even. You may use color cubes to help.

13. 17 _____   14. 36 _____   15. 15 _____

(Lesson 13) Use any strategy to solve.

16. Hunter wants to take a picture of his class. There are 24 students in his class. He wants them to stand in equal rows. What are all the ways he could arrange them?

_____

_____

(Lesson 14) Solve. You may use color cubes to help.

17. Each box A has 4 cubes inside. How many cubes can be in box B?

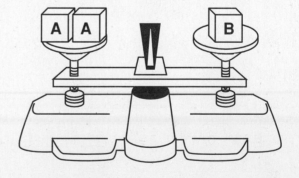

_____

(Mixed Review) Multiply.

18. 6 × 8 = _____   19. 9 × 9 = _____

20. 5 × 7 = _____   21. 4 × 8 = _____

Cumulative Review

(Chapter 2 Lesson 5) Make a list or use any strategy to solve.

1. Chelsea sells flower bulbs to gardeners.
   She has 48 bulbs that can be packed in boxes of
   8 or 4. How many ways can she pack the bulbs? _____

Boxes of 8:						
Boxes of 4:						

(Chapter 6 Lessons 3, 4 and 8) Multiply.

2. $\begin{array}{r} 3 \\ \times\, 6 \\ \hline \end{array}$	3. $\begin{array}{r} 7 \\ \times\, 3 \\ \hline \end{array}$	4. $\begin{array}{r} 4 \\ \times\, 8 \\ \hline \end{array}$	5. $\begin{array}{r} 7 \\ \times\, 6 \\ \hline \end{array}$	6. $\begin{array}{r} 9 \\ \times\, 7 \\ \hline \end{array}$

7. $\begin{array}{r} 8 \\ \times\, 8 \\ \hline \end{array}$	8. $\begin{array}{r} 6 \\ \times\, 4 \\ \hline \end{array}$	9. $\begin{array}{r} 3 \\ \times\, 8 \\ \hline \end{array}$	10. $\begin{array}{r} 7 \\ \times\, 7 \\ \hline \end{array}$	11. $\begin{array}{r} 9 \\ \times\, 6 \\ \hline \end{array}$

12. $7 \times 8 =$ _____   13. $8 \times 6 =$ _____

14. $7 \times 4 =$ _____   15. $5 \times 6 \times 0 =$ _____

16. $2 \times 3 \times 8 =$ _____   17. $1 \times 7 \times 8 =$ _____

18. $2 \times 4 \times 3 =$ _____   19. $2 \times 2 \times 7 =$ _____

(Chapter 7 Lessons 6 and 7) Find each quotient.

20. $15 \div 3 =$ _____   21. $10 \div 5 =$ _____

22. $25 \div 5 =$ _____   23. $36 \div 4 =$ _____

24. $35 \div 5 =$ _____   25. $24 \div 4 =$ _____

26. $21 \div 3 =$ _____   27. $15 \div 5 =$ _____

28. $3\overline{)27}$ 29. $4\overline{)28}$ 30. $5\overline{)20}$ 31. $3\overline{)9}$

Exploring Solids

1. Color the figures with flat faces red.

2. Color the figures that roll blue.

Cube

Sphere

Rectangular Prism

Cone

Pyramid

Cylinder

3. Which figures were colored twice? _____

Name the solid figure that each object looks like.

4.

5.

6.

CEREAL

tissues

_____   _____   _____

7. What solid figure does a baseball look like? _____

8. What solid figure does a drum look like? _____

9. What solid figure does a book look like? _____

Name _____

Exploring Solids and Shapes

Name the shapes of the dotted faces on each solid figure.

1.

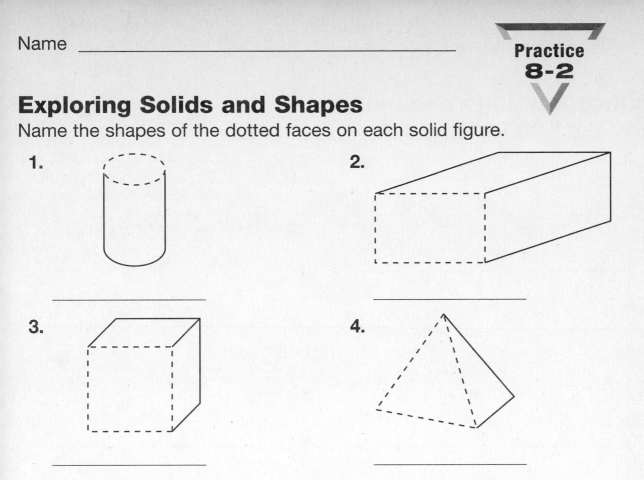

_____

2.

_____

3.

_____

4.

_____

Name the shape that each object looks like.

5.

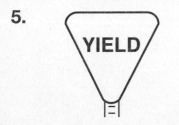

YIELD

_____

6.

_____

7.

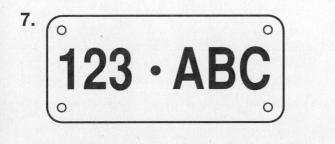

123 · ABC

_____

8.

SPEED LIMIT
20

_____

9. How many sides does a rectangle have? _____

10. How many sides does a circle have? _____

Lines and Line Segments

Write the name for each.

1. ●————————————●

_____

2. ←————————————→

←————————————→

_____

3. ●————————————→

_____

4. (crossing lines with arrows)

_____

5. ←————————————→

_____

6. ←————————————●

_____

7. How many endpoints does a line segment have? _____

8. How is a line segment like a ray? How is it different?

_____

_____

9. If two lines intersect, can they also be parallel? Explain.

_____

10. Draw a line segment.

11. Draw 2 parallel lines.

Name _____

Exploring Angles

1. Write the number 1 by the right angle.

2. Write the number 2 by the angle that is less than a right angle.

3. Write the number 3 by the angle that is greater than a right angle.

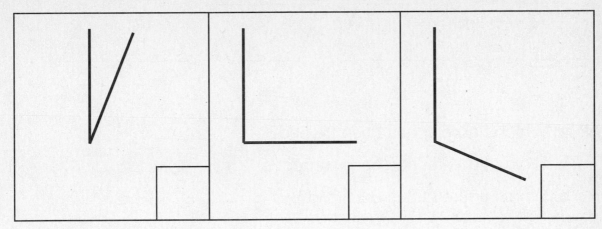

Write whether each angle is a right angle, less than a right angle, or greater than a right angle.

4.

5.

6.

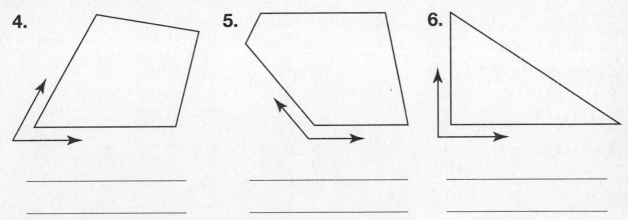

_____   _____   _____

_____   _____   _____

Write the number of right angles in each polygon.

7.

8.

9.

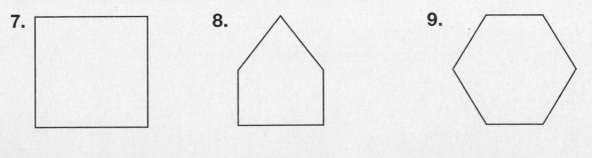

_____   _____   _____

Name _____

Exploring Slides, Flips, and Turns

Congruent figures have the same size and shape.

1. Color the figures that are congruent to the first figure blue.

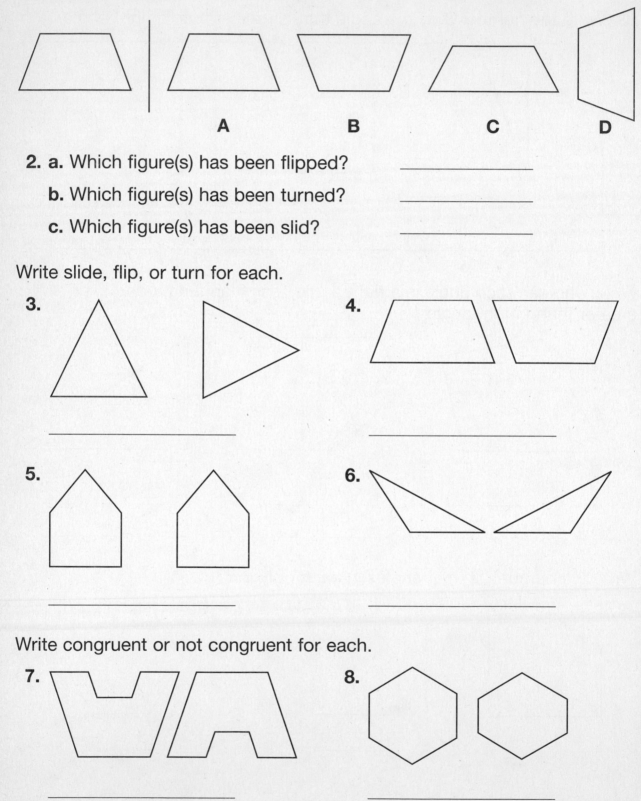

          A   B   C   D

2. a. Which figure(s) has been flipped?   _____

     b. Which figure(s) has been turned?   _____

     c. Which figure(s) has been slid?   _____

Write slide, flip, or turn for each.

3.

_____

4.

_____

5.

_____

6.

_____

Write congruent or not congruent for each.

7.

_____

8.

_____

Exploring Symmetry

A figure has a line of symmetry if you could fold the figure so both parts match exactly. Some figures have more than one line of symmetry.

1. Draw lines of symmetry on each figure. Color the figures that have only one line of symmetry.

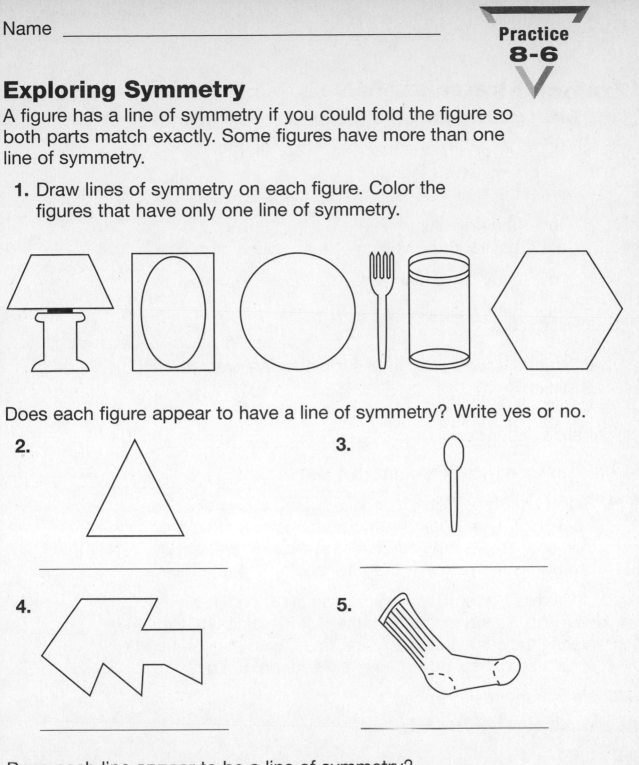

Does each figure appear to have a line of symmetry? Write yes or no.

2. _____

3. _____

4. _____

5. _____

Does each line appear to be a line of symmetry?
Write yes or no. If not, draw a correct line of symmetry.

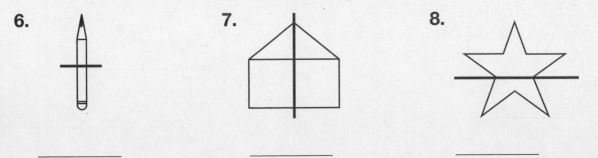

6. _____

7. _____

8. _____

Name _____

Analyze Strategies: Solve a Simpler Problem

See how many triangles you can find in this design.

1. a. How many small triangles
are in the design? _____

b. How many medium-sized
triangles are in the design? _____

c. How many large triangles? _____

d. How many triangles are
there in all? _____

e. What strategy did you use to solve the problem?

_____

_____

Use any strategy to solve each problem.

2. Sarah has three books to place together on her
bookshelf. One book is red, another is blue, and the third
is yellow. How many different ways can she arrange
the books if she wants the blue book in the middle? _____

3. Bryan has 79 football cards in his collection. He gives
seven to his friend and puts the rest in his album. He
places the same number of cards on each page. If he
uses nine pages, how many cards are on a page? _____

4. How many triangles can
you find in this triangular
design? _____

5. Four students are standing
in a line. Ned is to the right
of Helen. Carlos is the only
one between Keith and Ned.
Who is on the far left?

_____

Name _____

Review and Practice

Vocabulary Write true or false for each.

1. A cone has no faces.

   _____

2. A line segment is endless in both directions.

   _____

3. A right angle is an angle that forms a square corner.

   _____

4. A corner is where two or more edges meet.

   _____

(Lesson 1) Name the solid figure that each object looks like.

5.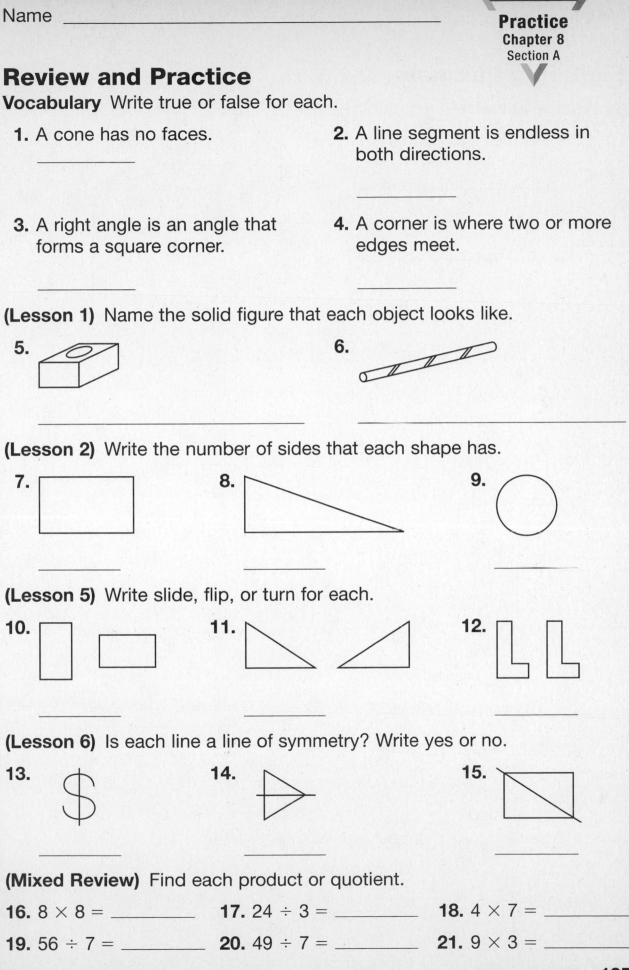

_____

6.

_____

(Lesson 2) Write the number of sides that each shape has.

7.

   _____

8.

   _____

9.

   _____

(Lesson 5) Write slide, flip, or turn for each.

10.

   _____

11.

   _____

12.

   _____

(Lesson 6) Is each line a line of symmetry? Write yes or no.

13.

   _____

14.

   _____

15.

   _____

(Mixed Review) Find each product or quotient.

16. $8 \times 8 =$ _____

17. $24 \div 3 =$ _____

18. $4 \times 7 =$ _____

19. $56 \div 7 =$ _____

20. $49 \div 7 =$ _____

21. $9 \times 3 =$ _____

Name _____

Exploring Perimeter

1. The perimeter is _____.

Find the perimeter of each.

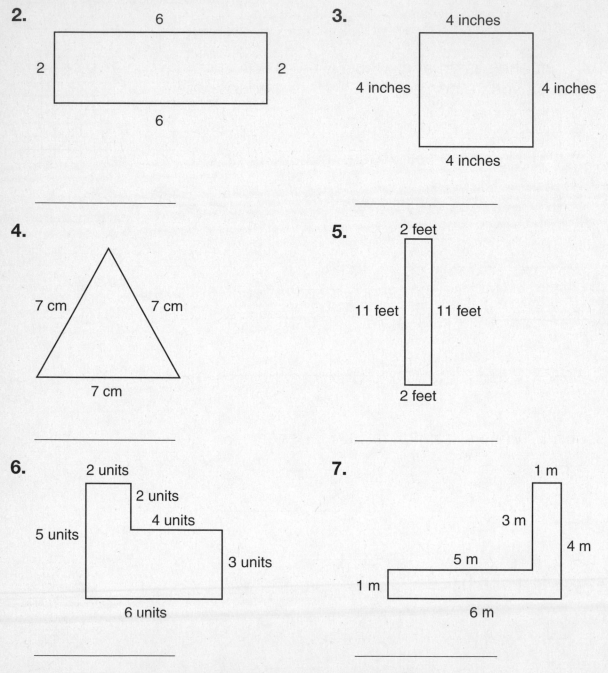

2.

6

2   2

6

_____

3.

4 inches

4 inches   4 inches

4 inches

_____

4.

7 cm   7 cm

7 cm

_____

5.

2 feet

11 feet   11 feet

2 feet

_____

6.

2 units

2 units

4 units

5 units

3 units

6 units

_____

7.

1 m

3 m

4 m

5 m

1 m

6 m

_____

Use grid paper. Draw a shape with each perimeter.

8. 8 units   **9.** 12 units   **10.** 4 units

11. 20 units   **12.** 26 units   **13.** 11 units

Name _____

Exploring Area

Find each area. Write your answer in square units.

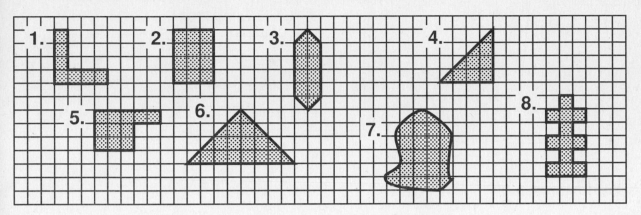

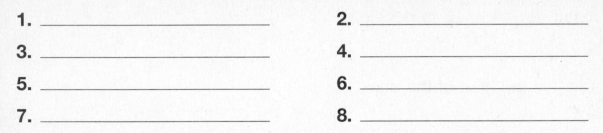

1. _____   2. _____

3. _____   4. _____

5. _____   6. _____

7. _____   8. _____

9. Use grid paper.

    a. Draw a rectangle with a perimeter that measures 10 units.

    b. What is the area of your rectangle?

    _____

    c. Draw a rectangle with the same perimeter but
    with a different area. What is the area of your rectangle?

    _____

10. a. What is the perimeter of the rectangle?

    _____

    b. What is the area of the rectangle? _____

    c. What happens to the perimeter if you halve each side?

    _____

    d. What happens to the area if you halve each side?

    _____

Decision Making

You want to move a desk
into your bedroom. Do
you have enough room?

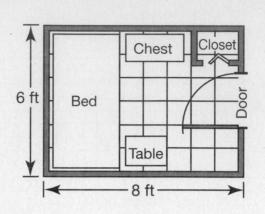

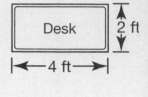

1. What do you know?

_____

2. What do you need to decide?

_____

3. What is the area of the desk?

_____

4. What else do you have to consider other then the area of the desk?

_____

5. Is there enough room for the desk?

_____

Find the area of the room and the couch. Decide if the
couch will fit in the room if no other furniture is moved.

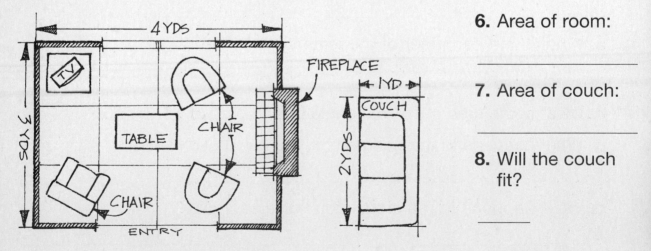

6. Area of room:

_____

7. Area of couch:

_____

8. Will the couch
fit?

Name _____

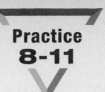
Exploring Volume

Write how many cubes are in each solid figure.

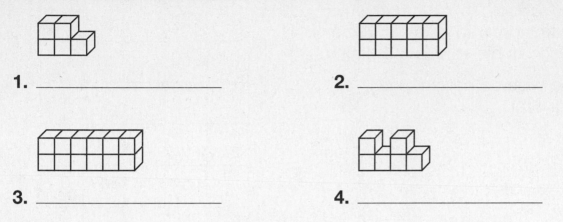

1. _____

2. _____

3. _____

4. _____

Find the volume of each. You may use cubes to help.

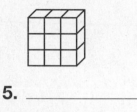

5. _____

6. _____

7. _____

8. _____

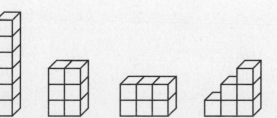

9. Is there a difference in the volumes of these solid figures?

Explain. _____

Coordinate Grids

Mr. Sanders has just begun teaching
at a new school. This is a grid which
Mr. Sanders drew to help him remember
where each of his students is sitting.

Write the ordered pair for each
student's seat.

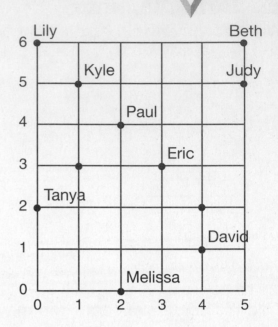

1. Kyle _____

2. David _____

3. Lily _____

4. Melissa _____

5. Beth _____

6. Tanya _____

Write the name of the student located at each ordered pair.

7. (3,3) _____

8. (5,5) _____

9. (0,2) _____

10. (2,4) _____

11. (5,6) _____

12. (2,0) _____

13. Are (0,2) and (2,0) at the same seat? Explain.

_____

14. To find Beth's seat from (0,0) how
    many spaces do you move to the right? _____

15. To find Paul's seat from (0,0) how
    many spaces do you move up? _____

16. Who is seated four places to the right of (1,5)? _____

17. Who is seated four places up from (0,2)? _____

18. Two new students join the class. Miranda sits at (1,3)
    and June sits at (4,2). Label these points on the grid.

Name _____

Review and Practice

Vocabulary Choose the correct word to complete each sentence.

Word List

cubic unit

coordinate grid

ordered pair

1. A(n) _____ is a graph used to locate points.

2. The unit used to measure volume is a

   _____ .

3. A pair of numbers used to locate a point

   on a grid is a(n) _____ .

(Lessons 8 and 9) Find the area and perimeter of each shape.

4.
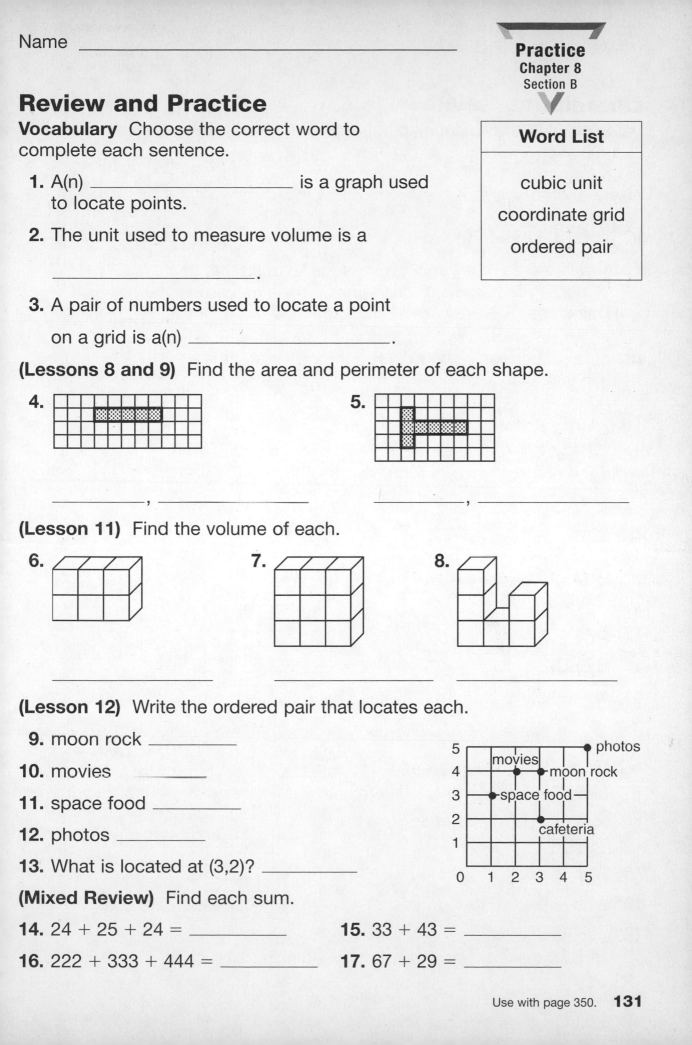

5.

_____ , _____   _____ , _____

(Lesson 11) Find the volume of each.

6.

7.

8.

_____   _____   _____

(Lesson 12) Write the ordered pair that locates each.

9. moon rock _____

10. movies _____

11. space food _____

12. photos _____

13. What is located at (3,2)? _____

(Mixed Review) Find each sum.

14. 24 + 25 + 24 = _____

15. 33 + 43 = _____

16. 222 + 333 + 444 = _____

17. 67 + 29 = _____

Cumulative Review

(Chapter 4 Lesson 15) Find each difference.

| 1. | $5.00
− 2.50 | 2. | $3.75
− 1.58 | 3. | $12.39
− 9.81 | 4. | $9.52
− 6.99 |

(Chapter 6 Lesson 9) Solve. Use any strategy.

5. Vickie wants to fry enough sausage links so that each of her 7 guests gets to eat 4 links. The links come in packages of 6. How many packages must she buy? _____

(Chapter 7 Lessons 10 and 11) Find each quotient.

6. $18 \div 6 =$ _____   7. $16 \div 8 =$ _____

8. $21 \div 7 =$ _____   9. $63 \div 7 =$ _____

10. $56 \div 8 =$ _____   11. $27 \div 9 =$ _____

12. $54 \div 6 =$ _____   13. $63 \div 9 =$ _____

14. $8\overline{)64}$ 15. $9\overline{)72}$ 16. $6\overline{)36}$ 17. $7\overline{)7}$

(Chapter 8 Lessons 8 and 9) Find the area and perimeter of each.

18.   19.

_____ , _____   _____ , _____

20. Draw a shape with an area of 14 square units.

21. Draw a shape with a perimeter of 14 units.

Exploring Multiplying Tens

Complete. You may use place-value blocks to help.

1. 5 groups of 7

$5 \times$ ☐ ones = ☐ ones

$5 \times 7 =$ ☐

2. 5 groups of 70

$5 \times$ ☐ tens = ☐ tens

$5 \times 70 =$ ☐

3. 5×1 ten = ☐ tens

$5 \times 10 =$ ☐

4. 2×4 tens = ☐ tens

$2 \times 40 =$ ☐

5. 3×5 tens = ☐ tens

$3 \times 50 =$ ☐

6. 2×5 tens = ☐ tens

$2 \times 50 =$ ☐

7. 3×6 tens = ☐ tens

$3 \times 60 =$ ☐

8. 4×6 tens = ☐ tens

$4 \times 60 =$ ☐

9. 7×1 ten = ☐ tens

$7 \times 10 =$ ☐

10. 3×8 tens = ☐ tens

$3 \times 80 =$ ☐

11. 4×4 tens = ☐ tens

$4 \times 40 =$ ☐

12. 2×7 tens = ☐ tens

$2 \times 70 =$ ☐

13. How can you use 7×6 to help you find 7×60?

_____

_____

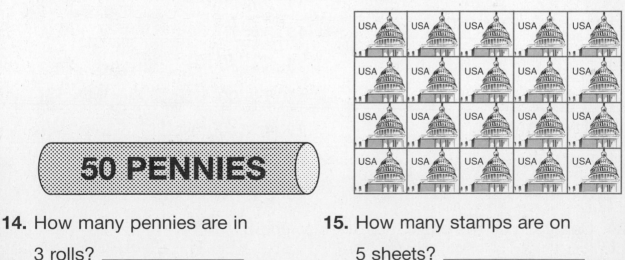

14. How many pennies are in 3 rolls? _____

15. How many stamps are on 5 sheets? _____

Exploring Multiplication Patterns

Complete.

1. 6 × 7 ones = ☐ ones

6 × 7 = ☐

2. 6 × 7 tens = ☐ tens

6 × 70 = ☐

3. 6 × 7 hundreds = ☐ hundreds

6 × 700 = ☐

4. 3 × 4 = ☐

3 × ☐ = 120

☐ × 400 = 1,200

5. 2 × 4 = ☐

☐ × 40 = 80

2 × 400 = ☐

6. 4 × ☐ = 20

4 × 50 = ☐

4 × ☐ = 2,000

7. 3 × 6 = ☐

3 × ☐ = 180

☐ × 600 = 1,800

8. 7 × ☐ = 28

7 × 40 = ☐

☐ × 400 = 2,800

9. 6 × 6 = ☐

☐ × 60 = 360

6 × 600 = ☐

Find each product using mental math.

10. 3 × 90 = _____

11. 3 × 800 = _____

12. 4 × 400 = _____

13. 2 × 70 = _____

14. 5 × 600 = _____

15. 6 × 800 = _____

16. 3 × 300 = _____

17. 5 × 90 = _____

18. 6 × 300 = _____

19. 4 × 500 = _____

20. 9 × 200 = _____

21. 7 × 700 = _____

22. 8 × 400 = _____

23. 5 × 800 = _____

24. Can you use the basic fact 3 × 8 to find 3 × 800?

_____

25. Can you use 5 × 7 to find 5 × 700?

_____

Name _____

Practice
9-3

Estimating Products

Estimate each product.

1. 3 × 32 _____   **2.** 7 × 820 _____

3. 5 × 46 _____   **4.** 2 × 350 _____

5. 8 × 67 _____   **6.** 6 × 865 _____

7. 3 × 523 _____   **8.** 4 × 628 _____

9. 4 × 233 _____   **10.** 9 × 58 _____

11. 5 × 797 _____   **12.** 6 × 84 _____

13. 3 × 124 _____   **14.** 5 × 99 _____

15. 7 × 280 _____   **16.** 8 × 241 _____

17. 6 × 890 _____   **18.** 2 × 916 _____

19. 9 × 760 _____   **20.** 4 × 675 _____

21. 3 × 210 _____   **22.** 9 × 63 _____

23. 4 × 334 _____   **24.** 6 × 912 _____

25. 7 × 489 _____   **26.** 8 × 38 _____

27. Estimate the product of 6 and 34. _____

28. Estimate the product of 7 and 569. _____

29. Estimate the product of 9 and 435. _____

30. Estimate the product of 8 and 750. _____

31. Estimate to decide if 6 × 856 is greater than or less than
7 × 535. Explain.

_____

32. The product of 6 and another number is about 240. Give
two numbers that make this sentence true. Explain.

_____

_____

Exploring Multiplication with Arrays

Complete the steps to find each product.

1. 3 × 14

   a. 3 rows of 10

     3 × 10 = ☐

   b. 3 rows of 4

     3 × 4 = ☐

   c. ☐ + ☐ = ☐

   d. 3 × 14 = ☐

2. 2 × 26

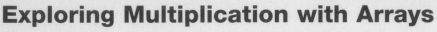

   a. 2 rows of 20

     2 × 20 = ☐

   b. 2 rows of 6

     2 × 6 = ☐

   c. ☐ + ☐ = ☐

   d. 2 × 26 = ☐

3. 4 × 23 = _____

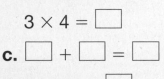

4. 5 × 13 = _____

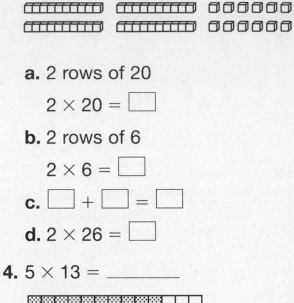

Find each product. You may use place-value blocks or grid paper to help.

5. 4 × 12 = _____   **6.** 6 × 13 = _____

7. 3 × 32 = _____   **8.** 4 × 17 = _____

9. 4 × 19 = _____   **10.** 2 × 47 = _____

11. 5 × 18 = _____   **12.** 3 × 28 = _____

13. 3 × 31 = _____   **14.** 2 × 39 = _____

Find the missing number. You may use grid paper or place-value blocks to solve.

15. 18 × _____ = 54   **16.** 12 × _____ = 84

17. 22 × _____ = 88   **18.** _____ × 19 = 57

19. 6 × 15 = _____   **20.** 5 × _____ = 70

Review and Practice

(Lesson 1) Complete. You may use place-value blocks.

1. 5×1 ten = ☐ tens

$5 \times 10 =$ ☐

2. 6×4 tens = ☐ tens

$6 \times 40 =$ ☐

3. 8×3 tens = ☐ tens

$8 \times 30 =$ ☐

4. 7×2 tens = ☐ tens

$7 \times 20 =$ ☐

(Lesson 2) Complete.

5. $5 \times 3 =$ ☐

$5 \times$ ☐ $= 150$

☐ $\times 300 = 1{,}500$

6. $6 \times$ ☐ $= 36$

☐ $\times 60 = 360$

$6 \times$ ☐ $= 3{,}600$

Find each product using mental math.

7. $7 \times 50 =$ _____

8. $9 \times 600 =$ _____

9. $80 \times 9 =$ _____

10. $400 \times 8 =$ _____

(Lesson 3) Estimate each product.

11. 8×56 _____

12. 33×5 _____

13. 3×299 _____

14. 6×419 _____

15. Melissa collects stamps. She mounts them on pages that hold 63 stamps. About how many stamps will 6 pages hold?

_____

(Lesson 4) Find each product. You may use place-value blocks or grid paper to help.

16. $6 \times 12 =$ _____

17. $3 \times 37 =$ _____

18. $5 \times 27 =$ _____

19. $4 \times 27 =$ _____

(Mixed Review) Add or subtract.

20.
$$\begin{array}{r} 361 \\ +839 \\ \hline \end{array}$$

21.
$$\begin{array}{r} 308 \\ -149 \\ \hline \end{array}$$

22.
$$\begin{array}{r} 917 \\ -579 \\ \hline \end{array}$$

23.
$$\begin{array}{r} 608 \\ +\ 55 \\ \hline \end{array}$$

Multiplying: Partial Products

Find each product.

1.
```
  1 5
×   3
  1 5
 □□
 □□
```

2.
```
  7 2
×   2
   □
 1 4 0
□□□
```

3.
```
  2 1
×   7
    □
□□□
□□□
```

4.
```
  1 3
×   6
 □□
 □□
 □□
```

5.
```
  3 9
×   7
 □□
□□□
□□□
```

6.
```
  4 2
×   6
 □□
□□□
□□□
```

7.
```
  6 7
×   7
 □□
□□□
□□□
```

8.
```
  5 3
×   5
 □□
□□□
□□□
```

9. 43 × 5 = _____

10. 64 × 3 = _____

11. 88 × 7 = _____

12. 39 × 4 = _____

13. 67 × 8 = _____

14. 37 × 6 = _____

15. 45 × 4 = _____

16. 69 × 2 = _____

17. 36 × 2 = _____

18. 84 × 5 = _____

19. 18 × 6 = _____

20. 23 × 9 = _____

21. Explain why 9 × 34 is the same as 270 + 36.

_____

22. How can you tell that 7 × 23 will be at least 3 digits?

_____

_____

23. Alexis says, "The product of 5 and 47 is less than 200."
Is she right? Explain.

_____

Multiplying 2-Digit Numbers

Find each product. Estimate to check.

1. 37
   × 2

2. 43
   × 7

3. 28
   × 3

4. 56
   × 5

5. 29
   × 3

6. 72
   × 6

7. 35
   × 7

8. 92
   × 6

9. 24
   × 8

10. 53
    × 5

11. 82
    × 3

12. 47
    × 6

13. 19
    × 8

14. 37
    × 9

15. 62
    × 4

16. 90
    × 7

17. $53 \times 5 =$ _____

18. $37 \times 3 =$ _____

19. $42 \times 8 =$ _____

20. $38 \times 7 =$ _____

21. Find the product of 17 and 9. _____

22. Find the product of 44 and 5. _____

23. Multiply 19 by 8. _____

24. Multiply 84 by 6. _____

25. Do you need to regroup ones to find the product of 42 and 3? Explain.

_____

26. Do you need to regroup to find the product of 34 and 3? Explain.

_____

27. How can you tell what the ones digit of the product of 38×7 will be without solving the whole problem?

_____

Multiplying 3-Digit Numbers

Find each product. Estimate to check.

1.   542
   ×   6

2.   374
   ×   3

3.   722
   ×   5

4.   256
   ×   7

5.   346
   ×   4

6.   117
   ×   8

7.   612
   ×   7

8.   739
   ×   2

9.   513
   ×   6

10.   757
   ×   3

11.   198
   ×   4

12.   209
   ×   8

13.   127
   ×   5

14.   508
   ×   6

15.   138
   ×   5

16.   377
   ×   9

17. $4 \times 311 =$ _____

18. $478 \times 8 =$ _____

19. $491 \times 5 =$ _____

20. $7 \times 219 =$ _____

21. $9 \times 106 =$ _____

22. $627 \times 6 =$ _____

23. Multiply 7 and 524. _____

24. Find the product of 378 and 6. _____

25. How could you use mental math to find 5×306?

_____

_____

26. How could you use mental math to find 3×122?

_____

_____

_____

Multiplying Money

Find each product.

1.	$1.20 $\times$ 5	2.	$0.65 $\times$ 7	3.	$3.24 $\times$ 6	4.	$1.75 $\times$ 5

5.	$0.49 $\times$ 8	6.	$3.19 $\times$ 4	7.	$2.39 $\times$ 3	8.	$4.12 $\times$ 5

9.	$2.25 $\times$ 3	10.	$1.52 $\times$ 6	11.	$2.22 $\times$ 6	12.	$4.33 $\times$ 7

13. $6 \times \$7.41 =$ _____

14. $\$2.29 \times 4 =$ _____

15. $\$1.19 \times 8 =$ _____

16. $9 \times \$0.79 =$ _____

17. $\$5.25 \times 4 =$ _____

18. $7 \times \$3.50 =$ _____

19. What is the product of 5 and $7.44? _____

20. Multiply 6 and $0.72. _____

21. Is $0.32 the same amount as 32¢? _____

22. Mindy multiplied $1.37 and 4. She recorded $5.48.

   Is she correct? _____

23. If you bought 9 cans of juice for 72¢ each, would you
   spend more than $5.00? Explain.

   _____

24. Ralph multiplied $2.69 and 5. He recorded $1345. Is he
   correct?

   _____

Mental Math

Find each product using mental math.

1. 42 × 3   **2.** 26 × 2   **3.** 14 × 6   **4.** 23 × 5

_____   _____   _____   _____

5. 32 × 8   **6.** 17 × 9   **7.** 37 × 3   **8.** 19 × 4

_____   _____   _____   _____

9. 21 × 6   **10.** 44 × 3   **11.** 53 × 4   **12.** 63 × 2

_____   _____   _____   _____

13. Multiply 6 and 47. _____

14. What is the product of 92 and 7. _____

15. If you know 30 × 4 = 120, how could you solve 36 × 4 mentally?

_____

16. If you know 30 × 3 = 90, how could you solve 29 × 3 mentally?

_____

17. What are two ways you could use mental math to find the product of 57 and 2?

_____

Analyze Strategies: Make a Table

1. This summer, a new 20-story hospital was built downtown. Electricians worked quickly to put in wiring in the building. After one week, 4 floors had wiring. After two weeks, 8 floors had wiring. After three weeks, 12 floors had wiring.

   a. Fill in the table to show what you know.

Week	1	2	3	4	5
Floors Wired	4				

   b. What multiplication pattern can help you complete the table?

   _____

   _____

   c. If the electricians continued to work at the same speed, how many weeks did it take them to put in wire in all 20 floors? _____

2. If it takes Ginny 7 minutes to ride 1 mile on her bike, how long would it take her to ride 6 miles? _____

3. If Todd can throw 20 curve balls in one minute, how many curve balls could he throw in 4 minutes? _____

4. Shea is decorating a frame. She has 4 rubber stamps she could use. They are a leaf, a ladybug, a flower, and a bee. She wants to make a design with 2 rubber stamps. How many choices does she have? _____

5. Eduardo has a red shirt, a blue shirt, and a white shirt, black trousers and blue jeans. How many different outfits can he make? _____

Name _____

Review and Practice

(Lessons 5–8) Find each product.

1. 43×7
2. 23×3
3. 93×6
4. 62×4

5. 308×4
6. 611×8
7. 980×4
8. 237×7

9. $\$6.18 \times 9$
10. $\$1.23 \times 6$
11. $\$0.11 \times 4$
12. $\$4.56 \times 3$

13. Sheila has 5 packets of raisins. Each packet contains 214 raisins. About how many raisins does Sheila have in all?

_____

14. Jack buys 4 tickets to a concert. Each ticket costs $4.89. How much does Jack spend?

_____

(Lesson 9) Use mental math to find each product.

15. $34 \times 5 = $ _____
16. $82 \times 3 = $ _____

17. $38 \times 4 = $ _____
18. $72 \times 4 = $ _____

(Lesson 10) Use any strategy to solve.

19. Kerim is saving money to buy a present. The first week he saves $1. The next week he saves $3. The third week he saves $5. If this pattern continues, how many more weeks will it be until he saves $25 in all? _____

(Mixed Review) Find each quotient.

20. $56 \div 8 = $ _____
21. $48 \div 6 = $ _____

22. $63 \div 9 = $ _____
23. $45 \div 5 = $ _____

Name _____

Exploring Division Patterns

Find the quotients. Use basic facts and place-value patterns
to help you divide mentally.

1. 8 ones ÷ 2 = _____ ones

8 ÷ 2 = _____

8 tens ÷ 2 = _____ tens

80 ÷ 2 = _____

8 hundreds ÷ 2 =

_____ hundreds

800 ÷ 2 = _____

2. 9 ones ÷ 3 = _____ ones

9 ÷ 3 = _____

9 tens ÷ 3 = _____ tens

90 ÷ 3 = _____

9 hundreds ÷ 3 =

_____ hundreds

900 ÷ 3 = _____

Complete.

3. 7 ÷ 7 = _____

70 ÷ _____ = 10

_____ ÷ 7 = 100

5. 8 ÷ 4 = _____

80 ÷ _____ = 20

_____ ÷ 4 = 200

4. 8 ÷ 2 = _____

_____ ÷ 2 = 40

_____ ÷ 2 = 400

6. 10 ÷ 2 = _____

100 ÷ _____ = 50

_____ ÷ 2 = 500

Find each quotient using mental math.

7. 800 ÷ 2 = _____

9. 200 ÷ 4 = _____

11. 210 ÷ 7 = _____

8. 90 ÷ 9 = _____

10. 270 ÷ 3 = _____

12. 360 ÷ 6 = _____

13. How can you use 16 ÷ 4 = 4 to help you find 160 ÷ 4?

_____

_____

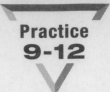

Estimating Quotients

Estimate each quotient.

1. 25 ÷ 6 _____   **2.** 35 ÷ 4 _____

3. 17 ÷ 4 _____   **4.** 29 ÷ 4 _____

5. 31 ÷ 8 _____   **6.** 19 ÷ 6 _____

7. 20 ÷ 3 _____   **8.** 14 ÷ 5 _____

9. 35 ÷ 6 _____   **10.** 39 ÷ 8 _____

11. 13 ÷ 6 _____   **12.** 65 ÷ 8 _____

13. 10 ÷ 3 _____   **14.** 11 ÷ 5 _____

15. 13 ÷ 4 _____   **16.** 73 ÷ 9 _____

17. Estimate the quotient of 25 ÷ 3. _____

18. Estimate the quotient of 41 ÷ 5. _____

19. What basic division fact can you use to help you estimate the quotient of 14 ÷ 5? Explain.

_____

_____

20. Is the quotient of 49 ÷ 6 greater than or less than 8? Explain.

_____

_____

21. Is the quotient of 53 ÷ 9 greater than or less than 6? Explain.

_____

_____

Exploring Division with Remainders

Find each quotient and remainder. You may use counters to help you.

1. 2)13

2. 8)29

3. 5)33

4. 4)25

5. 3)17

6. 6)21

7. 7)18

8. 5)28

9. 6)55

10. 5)16

11. 7)47

12. 3)26

13. Catherine says, "If I have 19 strawberries, I can give myself and 3 friends each 5 strawberries." Do you agree or disagree?

_____

14. Kim says, "If I need 25 granny-squares for a quilt, I can knit 8 squares a week for 3 weeks." Do you agree or disagree?

_____

15. Stefan was packing books into boxes. He had 8 boxes that would each hold 4 books. Stefan had 33 books. How many would not fit into the boxes?

_____

16. Robin is putting photographs into an album. He can fit 7 photographs onto a page. The album has 7 pages and Robin has 53 photographs. How many will not fit in the album?

_____

Dividing

Find each quotient and remainder.

1. $2\overline{)15}$ **2.** $4\overline{)23}$ **3.** $8\overline{)56}$ **4.** $5\overline{)43}$

5. $6\overline{)25}$ **6.** $9\overline{)48}$ **7.** $6\overline{)56}$ **8.** $4\overline{)33}$

9. $42 \div 7 =$ _____   **10.** $70 \div 8 =$ _____

11. $51 \div 8 =$ _____   **12.** $26 \div 3 =$ _____

13. $22 \div 8 =$ _____   **14.** $61 \div 7 =$ _____

15. $35 \div 9 =$ _____   **16.** $48 \div 6 =$ _____

17. $47 \div 5 =$ _____   **18.** $34 \div 8 =$ _____

19. Divide 55 by 7. _____   **20.** Divide 66 by 8. _____

21. Divide 44 by 6. _____   **22.** Divide 33 by 4. _____

23. Divide 22 by 5. _____   **24.** Divide 88 by 9. _____

25. 12 volunteers will paint 4 walls. How many
volunteers should work on each wall? _____

26. Suppose you want at least 15 rolls of film for
your vacation. How many 4-roll packages
should you buy? _____

27. How many traffic lights can you fill with a
case of 24 light bulbs? (There are 3 lights
on each traffic light.) _____

28. How many take-out boxes can you fill from
a crate of 50 muffins if there are 6 muffins
per take-out box? _____

29. Suppose 1 bottle of juice serves 5 people. How
many bottles will you need for 27 people? _____

Name  _____

Decision Making

You are planning a race. You need a water station every 3
miles. How many water stations will you need if the race is:

1. 12 miles long? _____

2. 21 miles long? _____

3. 15 miles long? _____

4. 18 miles long? _____

5. 24 miles long? _____

6. 30 miles long? _____

7. 26 miles long? _____

8. 20 miles long? _____

9. There are 36 runners in your race. They must be divided
into equal starting groups. Find 3 different ways to divide
36 runners into equal groups.

    a. _____ groups of _____ = 36

    b. _____ groups of _____ = 36

    c. _____ groups of _____ = 36

10. What if there are only 12 runners? Find 3 different ways
to divide 12 runners into equal groups.

    a. _____ groups of _____ = 12

    b. _____ groups of _____ = 12

    c. _____ groups of _____ = 12

Review and Practice

Vocabulary Underline the term that will complete the sentence correctly.

1. The (quotient, product) is the answer to a division problem.

2. The (quotient, remainder) is the number left over after dividing.

(Lesson 11) Use mental math to find each quotient.

3. 300 ÷ 6 = _____   **4.** 320 ÷ 8 = _____

5. 630 ÷ 7 = _____   **6.** 160 ÷ 4 = _____

7. Sarah's family is going on a 120-minute walk. They stop to rest 3 times. How often to they stop to rest?

_____

(Lesson 12) Estimate each quotient.

8. 31 ÷ 5 = _____   **9.** 46 ÷ 9 = _____

10. 19 ÷ 3 = _____   **11.** 52 ÷ 7 = _____

(Lessons 13 and 14) Find each quotient and remainder.

12. $2\overline{)9}$ **13.** $6\overline{)43}$ **14.** $4\overline{)29}$ **15.** $5\overline{)47}$

16. 69 ÷ 9 = _____   **17.** 58 ÷ 7 = _____

18. A bottle holds 9 ounces. How many bottles are needed to hold 57 ounces? Will all the bottles be full? Explain.

_____

_____

(Mixed Review) Add or subtract.

19.	**20.**	**21.**	**22.**
1 3 5	5 0 4	3 7 9	8 0 3
+ 2 2 2	− 2 4 3	− 8 4	+ 5 9

Cumulative Review

(Chapter 7 Lesson 9) Write which operation you would use. Then solve.

1. Mickey bought a dog collar for $5.95. He also
bought a 4-pound bag of dog food for $6.19.
How much money did he spend? _____

(Chapter 8 Lesson 4) Write whether each angle is a right
angle, less than a right angle, or greater than a right angle.

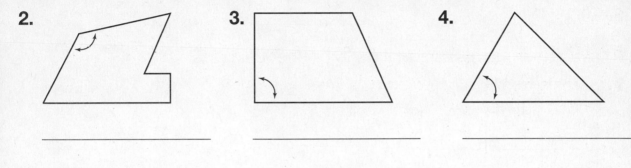

2.

3.

4.

_____   _____   _____

_____   _____   _____

(Chapter 8 Lesson 11) Find the volume of each shape. You
may use cubes to help.

5.

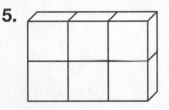

_____

6.

_____

(Chapter 9 Lessons 6 and 7) Multiply.

7.	**8.**	**9.**	**10.**
37	21	75	63
× 6	× 8	× 7	× 4

11.	**12.**	**13.**	**14.**
465	307	243	500
× 5	× 9	× 4	× 3

(Chapter 9 Lesson 14)

15. 4)29   **16.** 9)71   **17.** 3)28   **18.** 6)23

Name _____

Practice
10-1

Exploring Equal Parts

Tell how many equal parts.

1.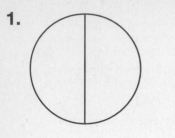

2.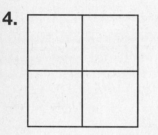

3.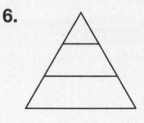

_____ _____ _____

Write whether each has equal parts or unequal parts.

4.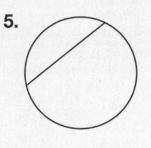

5.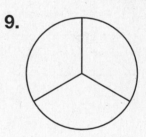

6.

_____ _____ _____

Name the equal parts of each whole.

7.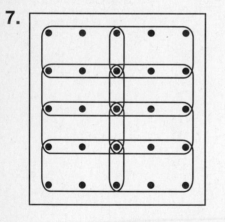

8.

9.

_____ _____ _____

Draw a picture to show each. You may use grid paper to help.

10. thirds

11. fourths

12. tenths

Naming and Writing Fractions

Write the fraction of each figure that is shaded.

1.

_____

2.

_____

3.

_____

4.

_____

5.

_____

6.

_____

Draw a picture to show each fraction.

7. $\frac{3}{8}$ shaded

8. $\frac{1}{10}$ shaded

9. $\frac{7}{12}$ shaded

10. $\frac{1}{6}$ shaded

11. $\frac{3}{5}$ shaded

12. $\frac{2}{4}$ shaded

13. Khalifa says "$\frac{2}{4}$ of the Maryland flag
has one design, and $\frac{2}{4}$ has another design."
Do you agree or disagree? Explain.

_____

_____

Exploring Equivalent Fractions

Complete. You may use fraction strips to help.

1. $\frac{1}{5} = \frac{\square}{10}$

$\boxed{\frac{1}{5}}$
$\boxed{\frac{1}{10}}\boxed{\frac{1}{10}}$

2. $\frac{1}{3} = \frac{\square}{6}$

$\boxed{\frac{1}{3}}$
$\boxed{\frac{1}{6}}\boxed{\frac{1}{6}}$

3. $\frac{2}{4} = \frac{\square}{8}$

$\boxed{\frac{1}{4}}\boxed{\frac{1}{4}}$
$\boxed{\frac{1}{8}}\boxed{\frac{1}{8}}\boxed{\frac{1}{8}}\boxed{\frac{1}{8}}$

4. $\frac{2}{5} = \frac{\square}{10}$

5. $\frac{1}{2} = \frac{\square}{8}$

6. $\frac{2}{3} = \frac{\square}{12}$

Write if the fractions are equivalent or not equivalent. You may use fraction strips to help.

7.

_____

8.

_____

9.

_____

Look for a pattern. Complete the next three fractions.

10. a. $\frac{1}{2}, \frac{2}{4}, \frac{3}{6}, \frac{4}{\square}, \frac{5}{\square}, \frac{6}{\square}$

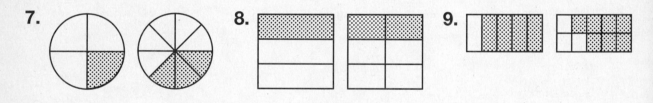

b. $\frac{3}{8}, \frac{6}{16}, \frac{9}{24}, \frac{\square}{32}, \frac{\square}{40}, \frac{\square}{48}$

c. $\frac{2}{5}, \frac{4}{10}, \frac{6}{15}, \frac{\square}{\square}, \frac{\square}{\square}, \frac{\square}{\square}$

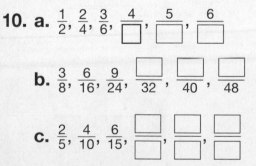

Exploring Comparing and Ordering Fractions

Place the fractions in order from greatest to least. You may
use fraction strips to help.

1. $\frac{1}{3}, \frac{1}{5}, \frac{1}{4}$ _____

2. $\frac{1}{3}, \frac{2}{3}, \frac{1}{2}$ _____

3. $\frac{3}{10}, \frac{2}{5}, \frac{1}{2}$ _____

4. $\frac{3}{4}, \frac{1}{2}, \frac{1}{6}$ _____

Place the fractions in order from least to greatest. You may
use fraction strips to help.

5. $\frac{1}{4}, \frac{1}{2}, \frac{1}{5}$ _____

6. $\frac{1}{2}, \frac{3}{4}, \frac{1}{3}$ _____

7. $\frac{2}{6}, \frac{2}{3}, \frac{1}{4}$ _____

8. $\frac{1}{10}, \frac{3}{5}, \frac{2}{8}$ _____

Compare. Write $<$, $>$, or $=$. You may use fraction strips to help.

9. $\frac{1}{2} \bigcirc \frac{5}{10}$

10. $\frac{1}{3} \bigcirc \frac{1}{5}$

11. $\frac{2}{8} \bigcirc \frac{2}{5}$

12. $\frac{3}{4} \bigcirc \frac{2}{3}$

13. $\frac{2}{4} \bigcirc \frac{3}{6}$

14. $\frac{2}{3} \bigcirc \frac{5}{6}$

15. $\frac{6}{10} \bigcirc \frac{2}{5}$

16. $\frac{1}{2} \bigcirc \frac{2}{3}$

17. $\frac{2}{12} \bigcirc \frac{1}{4}$

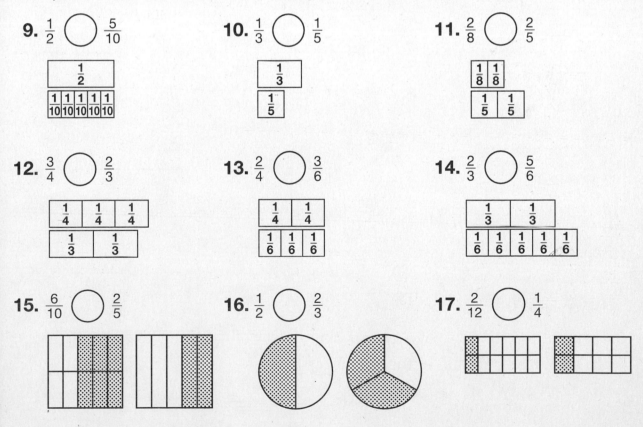

Name _____

Estimating Fractional Amounts

Estimate the amount that is shaded.

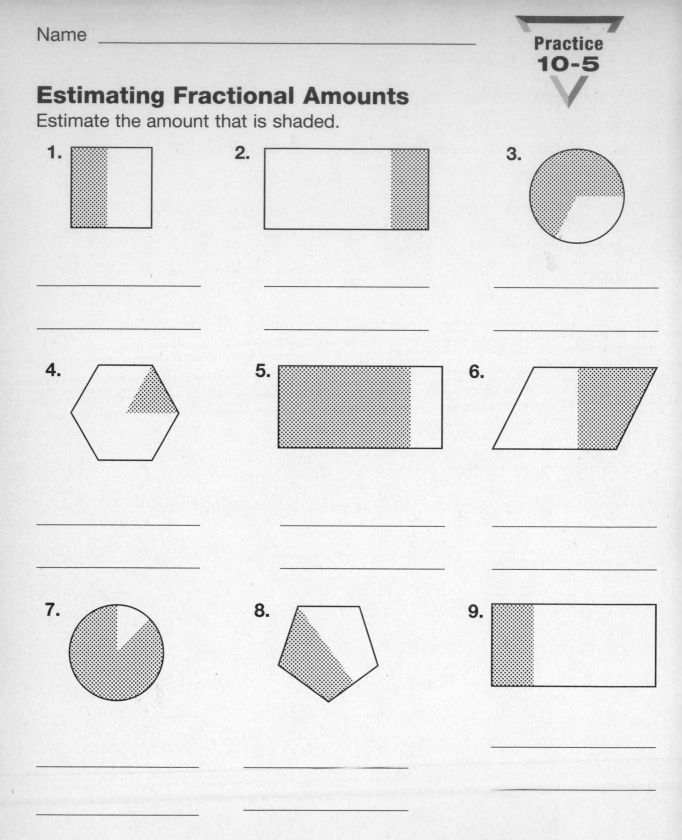

1.

2.

3.

_____

_____

_____

4.

5.

6.

_____

_____

_____

7.

8.

9.

_____

_____

_____

10. Tina needs about $\frac{2}{3}$ of a bar of clay
to make a dinosaur. Is there
enough clay left? Explain.

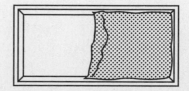

Review and Practice

Vocabulary Write true or false for each statement.

1. The numerator is the bottom number of a
   fraction and the denominator is the top number. _____

2. $\frac{3}{4}$ is a unit fraction. _____

(Lesson 1) Name the equal parts of each whole.

3. 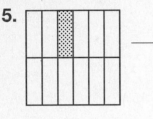 _____

4. 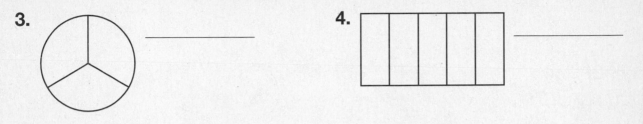 _____

(Lesson 2) Write the fraction of each figure that is shaded.

5. _____

6. _____

(Lesson 4) Compare. Write $<$, $>$, or $=$. You may use fraction strips to help.

7. $\frac{2}{5}$ ◯ $\frac{3}{10}$ 8. $\frac{1}{4}$ ◯ $\frac{2}{8}$ 9. $\frac{1}{3}$ ◯ $\frac{3}{6}$

(Lesson 5) Estimate each shaded amount.

10. 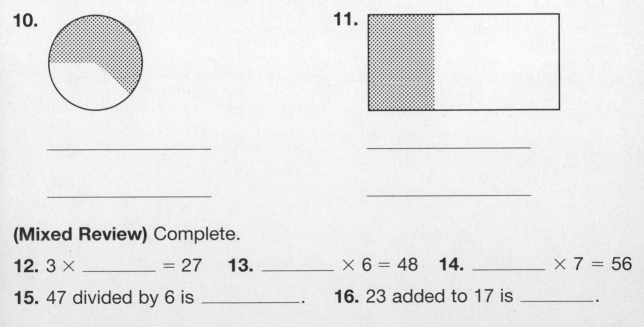   11.

_____   _____

_____   _____

(Mixed Review) Complete.

12. $3 \times$ _____ $= 27$ 13. _____ $\times 6 = 48$ 14. _____ $\times 7 = 56$

15. 47 divided by 6 is _____.   16. 23 added to 17 is _____.

Fractions and Sets

Write a fraction to tell what part of each set is circled.

1.

_____

2.

_____

3.

_____

4.

_____

Write a fraction to complete each sentence.

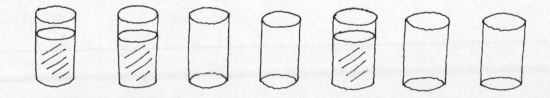

5. _____ of the windows have curtains.

6. _____ of the glasses are empty.

7. $\frac{5}{6}$ of Sean's 6 cats are female. How many are male?

_____

Name _____

Exploring Finding a Fraction of a Number

Complete.

1. To find $\frac{1}{4}$ of 12 divide 12 into _____ equal groups.

2. To find $\frac{1}{3}$ of 15 divide 15 into _____ equal groups.

Solve. You may use counters or draw a picture to help.

3. $\frac{1}{2}$ of 18 = _____

4. $\frac{1}{7}$ of 21 = _____

5. $\frac{1}{10}$ of 10 = _____

6. $\frac{1}{4}$ of 8 = _____

7. Find $\frac{1}{3}$ of 9. _____

8. Find $\frac{1}{4}$ of 20. _____

9. Find $\frac{1}{5}$ of 30. _____

10. Find $\frac{1}{6}$ of 24. _____

11. What fraction of the animals are:

    a. dogs? _____   **b.** cats? _____   **c.** birds? _____

12. Suppose an adult slept for $\frac{1}{4}$ of a 24-hour day.
How many hours did the person sleep?

_____

Mixed Numbers

Write a mixed number for each.

1.

_____

2.

_____

3.

_____

4.

_____

5.

_____

6.

_____

Answer each question.

7. Is there more or less than $1\frac{1}{4}$ pizzas? Explain.

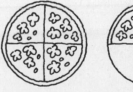

_____

_____

8. Leo said "$3\frac{3}{12}$ is the same as $3\frac{1}{4}$." Do you agree
or disagree? Explain.

_____

Exploring Adding and Subtracting Fractions

Find each sum or difference. You may use fraction strips or draw a picture to help.

1. $\frac{3}{5} + \frac{1}{5} =$ _____

2. $\frac{1}{4} + \frac{2}{4} =$ _____

3. $\frac{3}{5} - \frac{1}{5} =$ _____

4. $\frac{3}{4} - \frac{2}{4} =$ _____

5. $\frac{2}{6} + \frac{3}{6} =$ _____

6. $\frac{1}{5} + \frac{1}{5} =$ _____

7. $\frac{9}{12} - \frac{4}{12} =$ _____

8. $\frac{2}{9} - \frac{1}{9} =$ _____

9. $\frac{9}{10} - \frac{4}{10} =$ _____

10. $\frac{9}{16} + \frac{2}{16} =$ _____

11. $\frac{1}{4} + \frac{1}{4} =$ _____

12. $\frac{4}{7} - \frac{1}{7} =$ _____

13. $\frac{1}{3} + \frac{1}{3} =$ _____

14. $\frac{2}{6} - \frac{1}{6} =$ _____

15. $\frac{5}{8} - \frac{3}{8} =$ _____

16. $\frac{9}{12} - \frac{7}{12} =$ _____

17. Suppose you knocked over 9 out of 10 bowling pins. What fraction of the pins would still be standing?

_____

18. Suppose 5 out of 10 bowling pins were still standing. What fraction of the pins were knocked over?

_____

Decision Making

Your school won the city chess championship! Your team is having a party at your house and there are 8 players to feed.

You want at least 3 pieces of pizza per player. How many pizzas will you need if . . .

1. each pizza is cut into 6 pieces? _____

2. each pizza is cut into 8 pieces? _____

3. each pizza is cut into 10 pieces? _____

You want at least 2 glasses of juice per player. How many bottles of juice will you need if . . .

4. each bottle holds 6 glasses worth of juice? _____

5. each bottle holds 10 glasses worth of juice? _____

6. each bottle holds 4 glasses worth of juice? _____

7. Don't forget the victory cake! Can you think of 2 different ways to cut it so everyone gets the same number of pieces?

   a. _____ pieces

   b. _____ pieces

8. What if the coach wants cake, too? Draw pictures to show 2 different ways to divide the cake equally among 9 people.

   a.   b.

Review and Practice

(Lesson 6) Write a fraction that tells what part of the set is circled.

1.

_____

2.

_____

(Lesson 7) Solve. You may use counters or draw a picture to help.

3. Find $\frac{1}{4}$ of 24. _____

4. Find $\frac{1}{3}$ of 12. _____

5. Find $\frac{1}{5}$ of 20. _____

6. Find $\frac{1}{2}$ of 14. _____

7. Mitch has $18. He did put $\frac{1}{3}$ of the money in his savings account. How much did he put in his savings account? _____

(Lesson 8) Write a mixed number for each.

8.

_____

9.

_____

(Lesson 9) Find each sum or difference. You may use fraction strips or draw a picture to help.

10. $\frac{1}{6} + \frac{4}{6} =$ _____

11. $\frac{4}{5} - \frac{1}{5} =$ _____

12. $\frac{7}{9} - \frac{3}{9} =$ _____

13. $\frac{3}{8} + \frac{2}{8} =$ _____

(Mixed Review) Add or subtract.

14. $\begin{array}{r} 62 \\ + 33 \\ \hline \end{array}$

15. $\begin{array}{r} 98 \\ - 19 \\ \hline \end{array}$

16. $\begin{array}{r} 80 \\ + 73 \\ \hline \end{array}$

17. $\begin{array}{r} 82 \\ - 45 \\ \hline \end{array}$

Exploring Length

Estimate each length. Then measure to the nearest inch.

1. _____

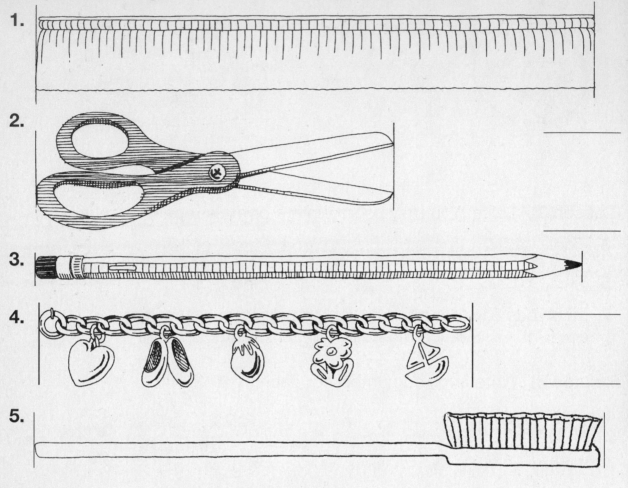

2. _____

3. _____

4. _____

5. _____

6. Suppose you need at least 5 inches of
wire for a project. Is this enough wire? _____

7. Measure the length of your thumb, your math book, and
your arm. Write each measurement in order from
greatest to least.

_____

8. Use a ruler. Draw a line to show each length.

   a. $2\frac{1}{2}$ inches

   b. 5 inches

   c. $6\frac{1}{4}$ inches

Name _____

Measuring to the Nearest $\frac{1}{2}$ Inch and $\frac{1}{4}$ Inch

Measure the length of each object to the nearest $\frac{1}{2}$ inch.

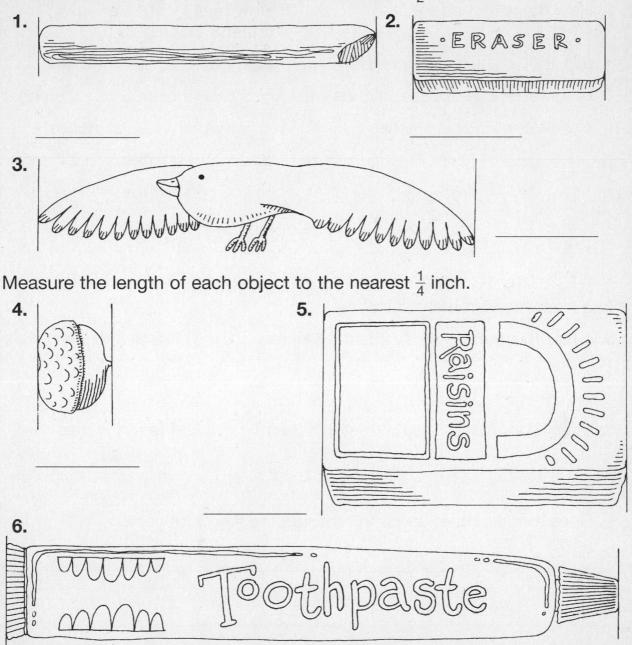

1.

2. ·ERASER·

_____   _____

3.

Measure the length of each object to the nearest $\frac{1}{4}$ inch.

4.

5. Raisins

_____   _____

6. Toothpaste

_____

7. You need to measure a pebble for a science project.
Does it make more sense to measure to the
nearest inch or $\frac{1}{2}$ inch?

_____

Exploring Length in Feet and Inches

You can multiply to write measurements in feet as measurements in inches.

1. How many inches are in 4 feet?

    a. 1 foot = _____ inches

    b. 4 feet = 4 × _____ inches

    c. 4 feet = _____ inches

2. How many inches are in 5 feet 8 inches?

    a. 1 foot = _____ inches

    b. 5 feet = 5 × _____ inches

    c. 5 feet = _____ inches

    d. _____ inches + 8 inches = _____ inches

    e. 5 feet 8 inches =

    _____

Write each measurement in inches.

3. 4 feet 8 inches

_____

4. 2 feet 11 inches

_____

5. 5 feet 5 inches

_____

6. 1 foot 9 inches

_____

7. 6 feet 3 inches

_____

8. 4 feet 4 inches

_____

9. Does it make more sense to measure the length of your pencil in feet or inches? Explain.

_____

_____

10. Does it make more sense to measure the length of your classroom in feet or inches? Explain.

_____

_____

Name _____

Feet, Yards, and Miles

Compare. Write $<$, $>$, or $=$.

1. 1,760 yd $\bigcirc$ 1 mile

2. 3 yd $\bigcirc$ 8 ft

3. 5 ft $\bigcirc$ 2 yd

4. 4,000 yd $\bigcirc$ 2 mi

5. 2 mi $\bigcirc$ 5,280 ft

6. 6 yd $\bigcirc$ 2 ft

7. 40 in. $\bigcirc$ 1 yd

8. 10 ft $\bigcirc$ 3 yd

9. 1 mi $\bigcirc$ 3,500 yd

10. 12 ft $\bigcirc$ 4 yd

11. 20 in. $\bigcirc$ 2 ft

12. 3 mi $\bigcirc$ 5,000 yd

13. 4,500 ft $\bigcirc$ 1 mi

14. 9 yd $\bigcirc$ 3 ft

Choose an estimate for each.

15. length of your bed _____ **a.** 1 yard

16. distance a person jogs _____ **b.** 1 foot

17. height of a desk _____ **c.** 2 yards

18. length of a football _____ **d.** 1 mile

19. Would it make sense to measure the distance from your home to school in feet? Explain.

_____

_____

20. Would it make sense to measure a bicycle in feet? Explain.

_____

_____

Name _____

Analyze Strategies: Use Logical Reasoning

Use logical reasoning to solve.

1. Help Peter figure out which soccer teams finished in first, second, third, and fourth place. The Wings finished in third place. The Hawks beat the Eagles and the Wings. The Tigers finished in last place.

_____

2. Ramon, Max, Jenna, and Maya are all on the same soccer team. Max is the youngest. Maya is older than Ramon. Jenna is 10 years old. If each player is either 9, 10, 11, or 12 years old, how old is each person?

_____

Use any strategy to solve.

3. Sean, Sharon, Ali, and Marie all have scored goals this season. Sharon has scored more goals than Ali and Sean. Sean has scored fewer goals than the three other players. Sharon has scored fewer goals than Marie. Order the players from greatest number of goals scored to fewest.

_____

4. I am an even number between 20 and 30. The sum of my tens digit and my ones digit is 6. What number am I? _____

5. I am an odd number between 50 and 60. The sum of my tens digit and my ones digit is 10. What number am I? _____

6. Mickey has 5 coins. The total value of the coins is $0.60. He doesn't have any pennies and only has 1 nickel. What coins does Mickey have?

_____

7. I am a number between 10 and 20. The difference between my digits is 0. What number am I? _____

Review and Practice

Vocabulary Write true or false for each statement.

1. Kevin can walk 1 mile in 1 second. _____

2. This paper is about 1 foot in length. _____

(Lesson 11) Measure the length of the object to the nearest inch.

3. _____

(Lesson 12) Measure the length of the object to the nearest $\frac{1}{4}$ inch.

4. _____

(Lesson 13) Write each measurement in inches.

5. 8 feet   **6.** 3 feet   **7.** 2 feet

_____   _____   _____

(Lesson 14) Compare. Write $<$, $>$, or $=$.

8. 2 feet $\bigcirc$ 22 inches   **9.** 2 yards $\bigcirc$ 6 feet

10. 5 yards $\bigcirc$ 140 inches   **11.** 3 miles $\bigcirc$ 21,120 feet

(Lesson 15) Use any strategy to solve.

12. Freda has 9 coins worth $1. Two are quarters. None are pennies. There is 1 more nickel than there are dimes. What coins does Freda have?

_____

(Mixed Review) Multiply or divide.

13. $6 \times 2 =$ _____   **14.** $32 \div 8 =$ _____

Name _____

Cumulative Review

(Chapter 4 Lesson 10) Subtract.

1.   673
  − 425

2.   315
  − 99

3.   830
  − 609

4.   749
  − 73

(Chapter 9 Lesson 8) Multiply.

5. $3.29
  ×   3

6. $3.10
  ×   4

7. $9.01
  ×   5

(Chapter 9 Lesson 13) Find each quotient and remainder. You may use counters to help.

8. $3\overline{)13}$ 9. $5\overline{)48}$ 10. $7\overline{)59}$ 11. $2\overline{)19}$

(Chapter 10 Lesson 2) Write the fraction of each figure that is shaded.

12.

13.

_____   _____

(Chapter 10 Lesson 4) Compare. Write <, >, or =. You may use fraction strips to help.

14. $\frac{1}{4} \bigcirc \frac{5}{8}$ 15. $\frac{3}{6} \bigcirc \frac{5}{12}$ 16. $\frac{2}{4} \bigcirc \frac{4}{8}$

17. $\frac{4}{5} \bigcirc \frac{5}{10}$ 18. $\frac{1}{2} \bigcirc \frac{2}{3}$ 19. $\frac{3}{4} \bigcirc \frac{8}{12}$

(Chapter 10 Lesson 9) Find each sum or difference. You may use fraction strips or draw a picture to help.

20. $\frac{6}{8} + \frac{1}{8} =$ _____   21. $\frac{2}{5} + \frac{3}{5} =$ _____

22. $\frac{6}{9} - \frac{3}{9} =$ _____   23. $\frac{7}{8} - \frac{5}{8} =$ _____

Name _____

Exploring Tenths

Any number in tenths can be written as a fraction or as a decimal.

Complete the table.

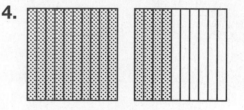

	Grids	Fraction or Mixed Number	Decimal	Word Name
1.			0.3	
2.				one and one tenth

Write the fraction and the decimal to name each shaded part.

3.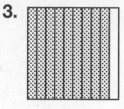

_____

4.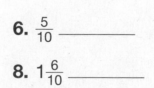

_____

Write each as a decimal.

5. eight tenths _____

6. $\frac{5}{10}$ _____

7. two and two tenths _____

8. $1\frac{6}{10}$ _____

9. Write each part of the circle as a fraction and a decimal.

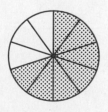

		Fraction	Decimal
a.	Shaded		
b.	Not shaded		

Hundredths

Write the fraction and the decimal to name each shaded part.

1.

_____

2.

_____

3.

_____

4.

_____

Write each as a decimal.

5. seventeen hundredths _____

6. nine hundredths _____

7. one and three hundredths _____

8. $\frac{22}{100}$ _____

9. fifty-one hundredths _____

10. $\frac{1}{100}$ _____

11. $2\frac{65}{100}$ _____

12. $1\frac{99}{100}$ _____

13. Is 0.70 greater than, less than, or equal to 0.7? Explain.

_____

14. What is the value of each bold digit?

    a. 0.8**4** _____

    b. 1.3**2** _____

    c. **3**.59 _____

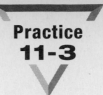

Exploring Adding and Subtracting Decimals

You can add and subtract decimals using pencil and paper.
You may use tenths grids to help.

1. Add 1.4 and 0.8.

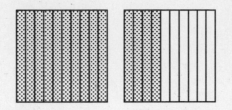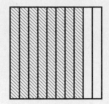

    a. Write the equation vertically in the space below.
    Line up the decimal points.

    b. Add tenths. Regroup if needed.
    Then add ones. What is the sum? _____

2. Subtract 1.6 from 2.5.

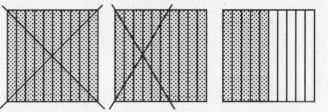

    a. Write the equation vertically in the space below.
    Line up the decimal points.

    b. Subtract tenths. Regroup if needed.
    Then subtract ones. What is the difference? _____

Find each sum or difference. You may use tenths grids to help.

3.	**4.**	**5.**	**6.**
3.3	1.9	8.6	6.2
+ 2.2	+ 4.5	− 3.4	− 4.8

7.	**8.**	**9.**	**10.**
0.7	2.2	5.8	1.5
+ 0.3	− 1.9	− 0.7	+ 1.6

Connecting Decimals and Money

Write each as a money amount.

1. $\frac{73}{100}$ of $1.00 _____

2. $\frac{39}{100}$ of $1.00 _____

3. $1\frac{15}{100}$ of $1.00 _____

4. $\frac{51}{100}$ of $1.00 _____

5. $2\frac{27}{100}$ of $1.00 _____

6. $\frac{98}{100}$ of $1.00 _____

7. sixty-six cents _____

8. forty-two cents _____

9. one dollar and ninety-one cents

_____

10. three dollars and three cents

_____

11. five dollars and twelve cents

_____

12. two dollars and eighty-eight cents

_____

13. fifty-four hundredths of $1.00

_____

14. three and thirty-seven hundredths of $1.00

_____

15. Complete the table.

		Fraction of $1.00	Decimal Part of $1.00
a.	$0.74		
b.	$0.02		
c.	$0.19		

Decision Making

You've decided to purchase a get-well gift for a friend who is ill. You want to go to the local mall to shop for the gift. Your goal is to find the perfect present and to be home by 5:00 P.M. You are bringing $10.00 with you. Below is a copy of the bus schedule for the bus which will take you to the mall. The bus stops on Carey Ave. right outside your house.

Leave Carey Ave.	Arrive Milford Mall	Leave Milford Mall	Arrive Carey Ave.
2:00 P.M.	2:15 P.M.	3:15 P.M.	4:00 P.M.
4:00 P.M.	4:15 P.M.	4:30 P.M.	4:45 P.M.

1. What information does the schedule give you?

_____

_____

2. When is the latest time you could leave the mall in order to get home on time?

_____

_____

3. How long does it take the bus to get to the mall from your bus stop on Carey Ave.? _____

4. If the one-way bus fare is $0.50, how much spending money do you actually have?

_____

5. You buy a shirt for your friend. It costs $8.00. How much money do you have left over to buy a snack? (Don't forget about the bus fare!)

_____

6. A muffin costs $0.60. Do you have enough money to buy one for your snack? _____ Could you buy two muffins?

_____

Review and Practice

Vocabulary Write true or false for each.

1. 85 cents is 85 tenths of a dollar. _____

2. A decimal uses place value and a decimal point to show tenths, hundredths, and so on. _____

3. The symbol used to separate ones from tenths in decimals is a comma. _____

(Lessons 1 and 2) Write the fraction and the decimal to name each shaded part.

4. **5.** **6.**

_____ ; _____   _____ ; _____   _____ ; _____

Write each as a decimal.

7. twenty-nine hundredths _____

8. $5\frac{3}{100}$ _____

9. two and four tenths _____

10. $\frac{8}{10}$ _____

(Lesson 3) Find each sum or difference. You may use tenths grids to help.

11.	**12.**	**13.**	**14.**	**15.**
3.8	8.3	2.6	8.5	4.7
+ 5.4	− 6.5	+ 3.4	− 5.8	+ 8.6

(Lesson 4) Write each as a money amount.

16. $\frac{16}{100}$ of $1.00 _____

17. $3\frac{29}{100}$ of $1.00 _____

(Mixed Review) Complete each number sentence.

18. 18 + _____ = 29

19. 57 − _____ = 21

20. _____ × 6 = 54

21. 56 ÷ _____ = 7

Exploring Centimeters and Decimeters

1. Write 1 cm below the item that measures 1 cm. Write
1 dm below the item that measures 1 dm.

a.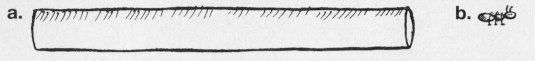

b.

_____   _____

Estimate the length of each object. Then measure to the nearest
centimeter.

2.

estimate _____

actual _____

3.

estimate _____

actual _____

Choose the best estimate for each.

4.

SIZE D
BATTERY

a. 5 cm _____

b. 1 dm

5.

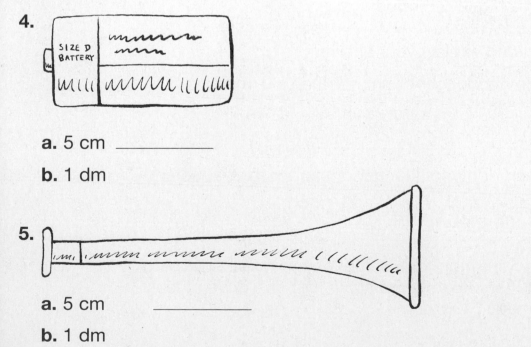

a. 5 cm _____

b. 1 dm

Meters and Kilometers

Match each with its estimate.

1. length of a hiking trail _____   **a.** 30 cm

2. width of a frying pan _____   **b.** 2 kilometers

3. height of a chimney _____   **c.** 3 m

Write whether you would measure each in cm, m, or km.

4. length of a nail _____

5. length of a large table _____

6. length of a hot dog _____

7. height of a mountain _____

8. length of a van _____

9. distance of a 20-minute train ride _____

10. depth of a lake _____

11. length of the Mississippi River _____

12. length of a highway bridge _____

Answer each and explain your answers.

13. Is a 87-cm rug longer or shorter than a 1-meter rug? Explain.

_____

14. Is a 300-cm-long sofa longer or shorter than a meter? Explain.

_____

15. Suppose your mom drove 800 meters to the shopping mall and then drove home again. Did she drive at least one kilometer? Explain.

_____

Name _____

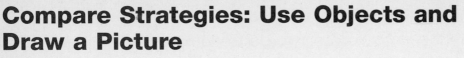
Compare Strategies: Use Objects and Draw a Picture

Use any strategy to solve.

1. A bus starts off on its route. At the first stop
   18 passengers get on. At the second stop
   10 more board, but 2 get off. At the third stop
   3 passengers get on and 1 passenger gets off.
   How many passengers are on board when
   the bus arrives at the fourth stop?   _____

2. The same bus departed the terminal at
   10:00 A.M. It arrived at the first stop 20 minutes
   later. It was delayed at this stop for 2 minutes.
   It took another 10 minutes for the bus to arrive
   at the second stop. At what time did the bus
   arrive at the second stop?   _____

3. The same bus arrived at the third stop at 10:45.
   How much time went by between the time it
   arrived at the second stop and the time it
   arrived at the third stop?   _____

4. Kim, Lisa, Ellen, and Martin have a jump rope
   contest. The jumper with the fewest misses
   wins. Martin wins with only 5 misses. Ellen has
   3 more misses than Martin. Kim misses twice
   as many times as Ellen. Lisa has 2 fewer
   misses than Ellen. Can you give the scores for
   Ellen, Kim, and Lisa? Who came in second?

   _____

5. Some students are making a chart to show
   how many students in the class were born in
   each month of the year. There are 22 students
   in the class. They find out that 1 student was
   born in January. Three times that many students
   were born in February. The months of March,
   April, September and October each had one
   less birth than the month of February. The rest
   of the students were born in the summer months.
   How many students had summer birthdays?   _____

Name _____

Review and Practice

Vocabulary. Choose the best word or words to complete each sentence. Use each word once.

meter	kilometer	centimeter	decimeter

1. A _____ is a metric unit equal to 1,000 meters.

2. A _____ is a metric unit equal to 10 _____s.

3. A _____ is a metric unit equal to 100 centimeters.

(Lesson 6) Match each with its estimate.

_____ **4.** 1 m   **a.** width of an audio cassette tape

_____ **5.** 1 dm   **b.** length of a pencil

_____ **6.** 1 cm   **c.** height of your teacher's desk

(Lesson 7) Write whether you would measure each in cm, m, or km.

7. a car trip _____   **8.** length of a marathon _____

9. length of a car _____   **10.** width of a book _____

11. height of a dog _____   **12.** height of a flag pole _____

(Lesson 8) Solve. Use any strategy.

13. A shelf at the grocery store had 15 loaves of bread on it. One shopper buys 3 loaves, another buys 5 loaves. The stock person restocks the shelf with 10 more loaves, then 3 more shoppers each buy 2 loaves. How many loaves of bread are on the shelf? _____

14. Maxine rode the elevator to the third floor, where she got off. She then climbed up 2 flights of stairs and got back on the elevator. She took the elevator down 3 floors. What floor is she now on? _____

(Mixed Review) Find each product.

15. $\begin{array}{r} 23 \\ \times\ 5 \\ \hline \end{array}$ **16.** $\begin{array}{r} 45 \\ \times\ 6 \\ \hline \end{array}$ **17.** $\begin{array}{r} \$3.14 \\ \times\quad 9 \\ \hline \end{array}$ **18.** $\begin{array}{r} 822 \\ \times\quad 3 \\ \hline \end{array}$

Cumulative Review

(Chapter 3 Lesson 10) Solve. Use any strategy.

1. The sum of 2 numbers is 61. The numbers are 5 apart. What are they? _____

2. The difference of 2 numbers is 10. The sum of the numbers is 14. What are they? _____

(Chapter 4 Lesson 11) Find each difference.

3. $\begin{array}{r} 807 \\ -\ 29 \\ \hline \end{array}$
4. $\begin{array}{r} \$306 \\ -\ 168 \\ \hline \end{array}$
5. $\begin{array}{r} 900 \\ -\ 824 \\ \hline \end{array}$

(Chapter 9 Lesson 14) Find each quotient and remainder.

6. $7\overline{)60}$ 7. $8\overline{)56}$ 8. $3\overline{)14}$ 9. $5\overline{)32}$

(Chapter 10 Lesson 6) Write a fraction to tell what part of each set is circled.

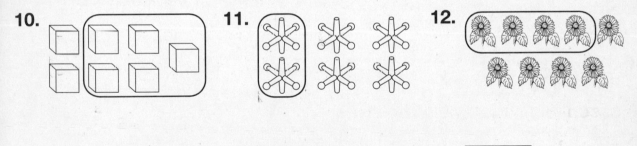

10. _____   11. _____   12. _____

(Chapter 11 Lesson 3) Find each sum or difference.

13. $\begin{array}{r} 3.6 \\ +\ 2.3 \\ \hline \end{array}$
14. $\begin{array}{r} 9.4 \\ -\ 6.8 \\ \hline \end{array}$
15. $\begin{array}{r} 0.9 \\ +\ 7.7 \\ \hline \end{array}$
16. $\begin{array}{r} 9.9 \\ -\ 1.6 \\ \hline \end{array}$

(Chapter 11 Lesson 4) Write each as a money amount.

17. $\frac{26}{100}$ of $1.00 _____

18. $4\frac{53}{100}$ of $1.00 _____

19. three dollars and five cents _____

20. seventy-two hundredths of $1.00 _____

Name _____

Exploring Capacity: Customary Units

Complete.

1. _____ cups = 1 pint

2. 4 cups = _____ pints = _____ quart

3. _____ cups = 8 pints = _____ quarts = 1 gallon

Circle the best estimate for each.

4.

a. 1 cup

b. 1 quart

c. 1 pint

5.

a. 1 cup

b. 1 pint

c. 1 gallon

6.

a. 1 quart

b. 1 pint

c. 1 gallon

7.

a. 1 pint

b. 1 quart

c. 1 cup

8.

a. 1 pint

b. 1 quart

c. 1 gallon

9.

a. 1 cup

b. 1 quart

c. 1 gallon

Compare. Use <, >, or =.

10. 6 pints ◯ 1 gallon

11. 2 pints ◯ 3 cups

12. 2 quarts ◯ 4 pints

13. 16 cups ◯ 3 quarts

14. Suppose you want to make pudding. The recipe calls for
4 cups of milk. You have 1 quart. Do you have enough
milk to make the recipe? Explain.

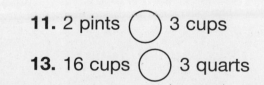

Measuring Capacity: Metric Units

Circle the better estimate for each.

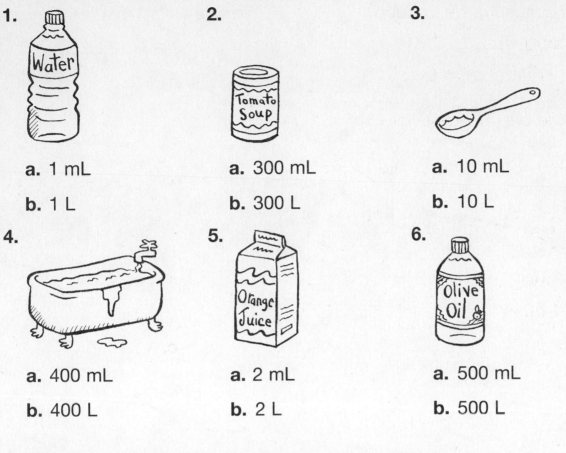

1.

a. 1 mL

b. 1 L

2.

a. 300 mL

b. 300 L

3.

a. 10 mL

b. 10 L

4.

a. 400 mL

b. 400 L

5.

a. 2 mL

b. 2 L

6.

a. 500 mL

b. 500 L

7. Does a jar of honey hold about 600 mL or 600 L? _____

8. Does a plastic jug of milk hold about 3 mL or 3 L? _____

9. Suppose you estimated that you have made about 2 liters of lemonade. How could you check your estimate?

_____

_____

_____

10. What kind of container might hold many liters of water?

_____

Name _____

Exploring Weight: Customary Units

Compare. Use <, >, or =.

1. 16 ounces $\bigcirc$ 1 pound **2.** 1 ounce $\bigcirc$ 1 pound

3. 18 ounces $\bigcirc$ 1 pound **4.** 12 ounces $\bigcirc$ 1 pound

Circle the better estimate for each.

5.

6.

7.

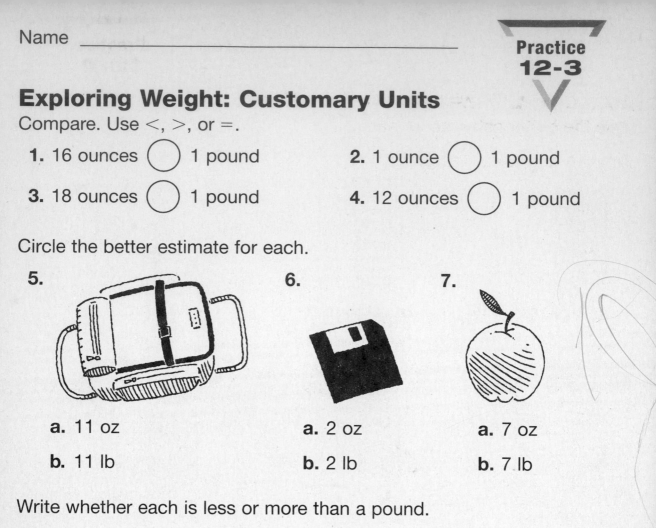

a. 11 oz **a.** 2 oz **a.** 7 oz

b. 11 lb **b.** 2 lb **b.** 7 lb

Write whether each is less or more than a pound.

8. **9.** **10.**

_____ _____ _____

11. Suppose a dog weighs 8 pounds. How many ounces

does it weigh? _____

12. Suppose a person's brain weighs about 3 pounds. How

many ounces does it weigh? _____

13. Complete the table.

Ounces	16	32		64	80	96
Pounds	1	2				

Name _____

Practice
12-4

Grams and Kilograms

Circle the better estimate for each.

1.

a. 2 g

b. 2 kg

2.

a. 560 g

b. 560 kg

3.

a. 15 g

b. 15 kg

4.

a. 100 g

b. 100 kg

5.

a. 4 g

b. 4 kg

6.

a. 50 g

b. 50 kg

7. an 8-year-old boy

a. 30 g

b. 30 kg

8. a china cup

a. 350 g

b. 350 kg

9. a pen

a. 5 g

b. 5 kg

9. Remy says, "The number of grams in 2 kilograms is 2 × 1,000."
Do you agree or disagree? Explain.

agree I do not know I am guessing

10. Which is heavier, a 3-kg rock or a 2,800-g rock? Explain.

3 kg rock I do not now I am guessing

Use with pages 492–493. **185**

Name _____

Temperature

Write the temperature using °C or °F.

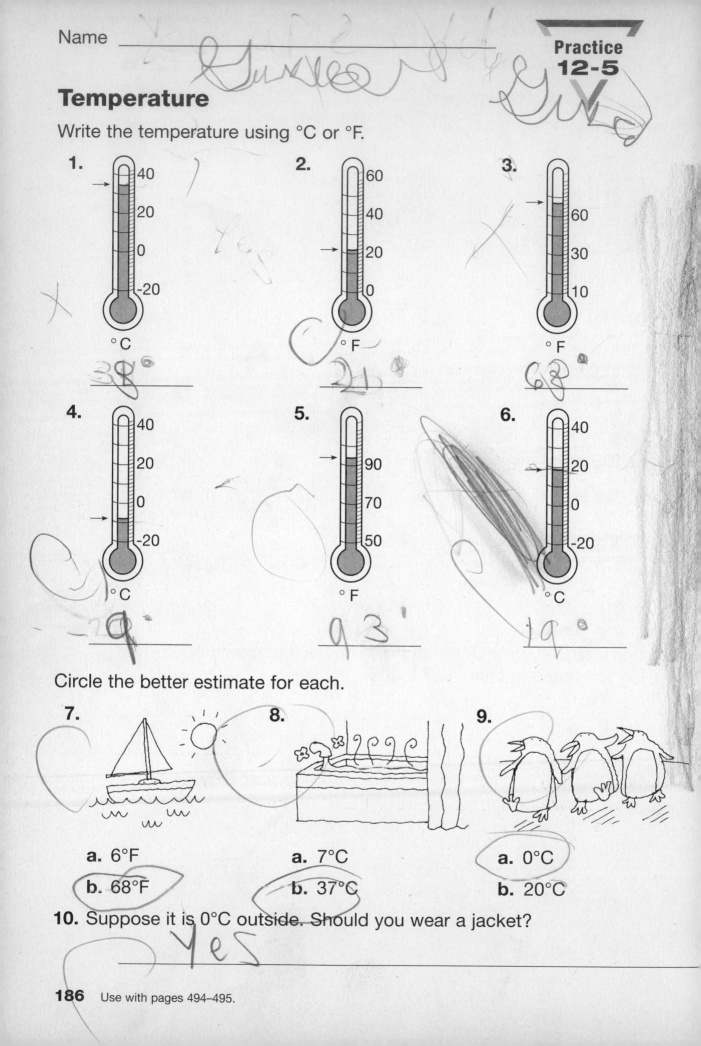

1. °C
    38

2. °F
    21

3. °F
    68

4. °C
    9

5. °F
    93

6. °C
    19

Circle the better estimate for each.

7. **a.** 6°F
    b. 68°F

8. **a.** 7°C
    b. 37°C

9. **a.** 0°C
    b. 20°C

10. Suppose it is 0°C outside. Should you wear a jacket?

_____ Yes

Name _____

Practice
12-6

Decision Making

You are going on a backpacking trip. This is what you plan
to take.

Item	Weight
backpack	3 lb
3 sweaters	1 lb each
1 canteen of water	2 lb 8 oz
2 pairs of pants	8 oz each
2 mess kits	8 oz each
3 flashlights	1 lb each
1 camera	2 lb
1 tape player	1 lb
4 cassette tapes	2 oz each
socks, t-shirts, etc.	2 lb

1. What will the total weight of your backpack be when you
pack all of these items?

_____

2. If you needed to make your pack 2 lb lighter, which
items would you remove? Why?

_____

_____

3. If you had room in your pack for 3 lb more, what would
you include? (Estimate the weight of the item if it is not
on the list.)

_____

_____

Review and Practice

(Lessons 1 and 2) Circle the best estimate for each.

1.

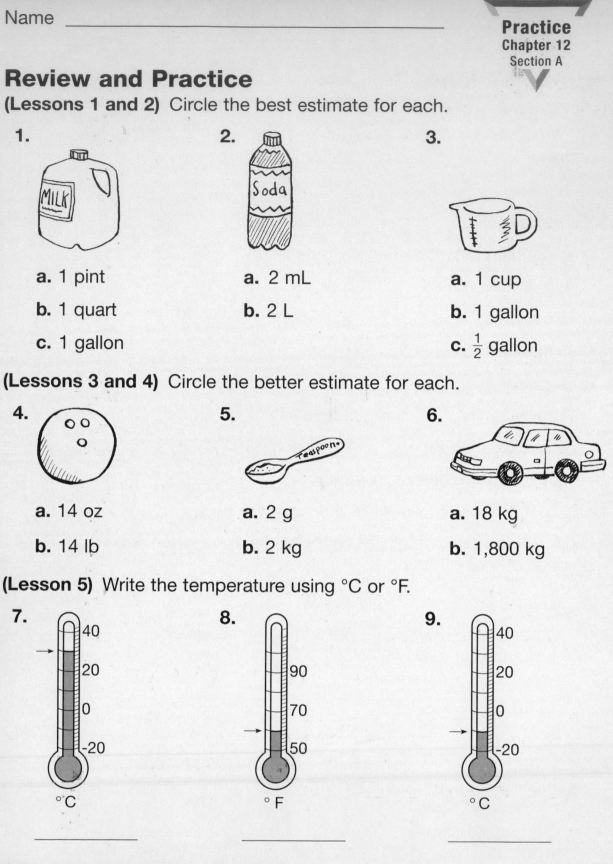

a. 1 pint

b. 1 quart

c. 1 gallon

2.

a. 2 mL

b. 2 L

3.

a. 1 cup

b. 1 gallon

c. $\frac{1}{2}$ gallon

(Lessons 3 and 4) Circle the better estimate for each.

4.

a. 14 oz

b. 14 lb

5.

a. 2 g

b. 2 kg

6.

a. 18 kg

b. 1,800 kg

(Lesson 5) Write the temperature using °C or °F.

7.

40
20
0
-20

°C

_____

8.

90

70

50

°F

_____

9.

40
20
0
-20

°C

_____

(Mixed Review) Add or subtract.

10.
   318
− 109

11.
   825
+ 117

12.
   700
− 283

13.
   421
− 89

Name _____

Exploring Likely and Unlikely

1. Match each statement on the left with the best answer on the right.

   a. There will be no Wednesday next week.   Certain

   b. There will be clouds
      in the sky tomorrow.   Unlikely

   c. It will snow in Florida this year.   Impossible

   d. The desert will be hot this summer.   Likely

Write whether each is impossible, possible, or certain.

2. An elephant will learn how to fly. _____

3. Many trees will lose their leaves this fall. _____

4. A person is sleeping somewhere. _____

Write whether each is likely or unlikely.

5. The 6 o'clock news on TV will start late today. _____

6. Milk will be served in school cafeterias. _____

7. Next week, all of the books in the library will be checked out.

   _____

8. Your hair will be the same color in five years. _____

9. Students in your class will do some homework tonight.

   _____

10. It will rain daisies and roses tomorrow. _____

11. Heather said, "It is likely that flowers will bloom this spring." Do you
    agree or disagree? Explain.

    _____

    _____

Exploring Predictions

1. Look at the spinner. List the possible outcomes of a spin. Complete the predictions with *more*, *fewer*, *all*, or *no*.

	Possible Outcomes	Predictions
		The pointer will land on dots _____ times. It will land on stripes _____ times.

Suppose you put these cubes in a bag. Predict which cubes you are more likely to pull out.

2.

_____

3.

_____

4.

_____

5.

_____

6. Would it be easier to guess the month or the day of the week that someone was born? Explain.

_____

_____

Name _____

Exploring Probability

Complete each sentence with a fraction that shows
probability.

1. 3 out of 8 students are wearing blue shirts. The probability that a
   student is wearing a blue shirt is $\dfrac{\square}{8}$.

2. 2 out of 8 students are wearing red shirts. The probability that a
   student is wearing a red shirt is $\dfrac{\square}{8}$.

3. 2 out of 8 students are wearing green shirts. The probability that a
   student is wearing a green shirt is $\dfrac{\square}{8}$.

4. 1 out of 8 students is wearing a yellow shirt. The probability that a
   student is wearing a yellow shirt is $\dfrac{\square}{8}$.

5.
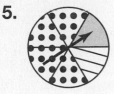

   a. grey: $\square$ out of 6 or $\dfrac{\square}{6}$

   b. striped: $\square$ out of 6 or $\dfrac{\square}{6}$

   c. dotted: $\square$ out of 6 or $\dfrac{\square}{6}$

6. 1 side of a plastic cube is orange, 2 sides are pink, and
   3 sides are purple.

   a. If you toss the cube, which color
      is most likely to land face up?   _____

   b. If you toss the cube, which color
      is least likely to land face up?   _____

7. A contest has the following 15 prizes: 1 trip to Hawaii,
   2 CD players, 3 pairs of hiking boots, 4 radios, and 5 posters.
   You have been told that you won one of the prizes.

   a. Which prize are you most likely to have won? _____

   b. Which prize are you least likely to have won? _____

Name _____

Exploring Fair and Unfair

1.

2.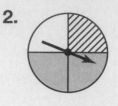

a. ☐ out of 4 equal sections are gray.

b. The probability of spinning gray is $\frac{\square}{4}$.

c. Is spinning gray likely?

_____

a. ☐ out of 4 equal sections are white.

b. The probability of spinning white is $\frac{\square}{4}$.

c. Is spinning white likely?

_____

3. Are the spinners shown in 1 and 2 fair? _____

Write whether each spinner is fair or unfair.

4.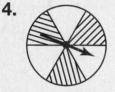

5.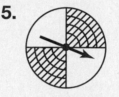

_____

_____

6.

7.

_____

_____

8. If there are 2 red cubes and 6 white cubes in a box, are the chances of picking a red cube likely, unlikely, or equally likely? Explain.

_____

9. There are 3 green and 3 blue cubes in a box. Are the chances of picking a green cube likely, unlikely, or equally likely to picking a blue cube? Explain.

_____

Name _____

Analyze Strategies: Work Backward

Work backward or use any strategy to solve each problem.

1. Kim must be at the airport at 8:00 A.M. She needs 45 minutes to shower, dress, and eat breakfast. She needs 1 hour to drive to the airport. She wants to allow an extra 30 minutes for traffic. She needs 8 hours and 45 minutes of sleep the night before her trip. What time should she go to sleep?

_____

2. Jody said, "I am thinking of a number. If I add 24 to the number, then subtract 6, then add 12, and then multiply by 2, I end up with 84." What number did Jody start with? _____

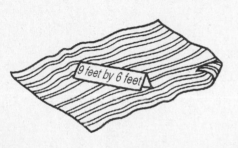

9 feet by 6 feet

3. Skyler has a large piece of blue fabric. She wants to make table napkins out of it. If each napkin requires 1 square foot of fabric, how many napkins can she make from the fabric? Use the drawing to help.

_____

4. Jason used the exercise machines at the gym. He worked on 2 machines for his arms. He skipped 5 arm exercises that he usually did because each of these machines was busy. Then he worked on his legs, using 6 machines. How many machines does Jason usually use?

_____

5. Derek used small rocks to border the garden. He used $\frac{1}{2}$ of the rocks to border the roses. Then he used 31 rocks to border the tulips and 25 to border the daffodils. He had 24 rocks left over. How many rocks did Derek start with?

_____

Name _____

Review and Practice

Vocabulary Match each with its definition.

_____ **1.** certain   **a.** able to happen

_____ **2.** possible   **b.** a guess about what will happen

_____ **3.** likely   **c.** sure to happen

_____ **4.** prediction   **d.** probably will happen

(Lesson 8) Suppose you put these letters in a bag. Predict which letter you are more likely to pull out.

5. _____   **6.** _____   **7.** _____

(Lesson 9) Complete.

8. striped: _____ out of 5 or $\dfrac{\square}{5}$.

9. dotted: _____ out of 5 or $\dfrac{\square}{5}$.

10. white: _____ out of 5 or $\dfrac{\square}{5}$.

(Lesson 10) Write whether each spinner is fair or unfair.

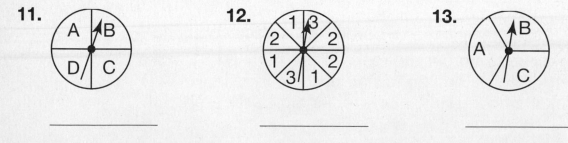

11. _____   **12.** _____   **13.** _____

(Mixed Review) Divide.

14. $3\overline{)19}$ **15.** $5\overline{)49}$ **16.** $8\overline{)47}$ **17.** $4\overline{)26}$

Name _____

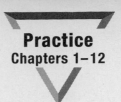
Cumulative Review

(Chapter 8 Lesson 2) Complete the chart.

	Shape	Number of Sides	Number of Corners
1.	triangle		
2.	circle		
3.	rectangle		

(Chapter 9 Lesson 9) Find each product using mental math.

4. $42 \times 5 =$ _____

5. $21 \times 6 =$ _____

(Chapter 10 Lesson 12) Measure the length to the nearest $\frac{1}{4}$ inch.

(Chapter 11 Lesson 6) Use a ruler to measure the perimeter to the nearest centimeter.

6. _____

7. _____

(Chapter 12 Lesson 5) Write the temperature. Use °C or °F.

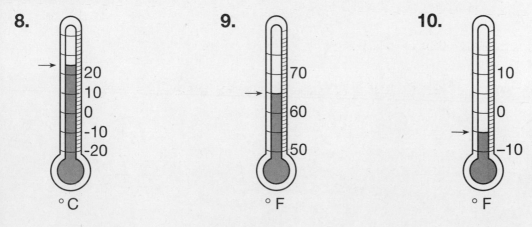

8. _____

9. _____

10. _____